Share Your Story

How to write and publish YOUR book

By

Joe B. Parr

JOE B. PARR

U.S. Copyright © 2016 1-xxxxxxxxxx by Joe B. Parr

First Edition

http://joebparr.com

All rights reserved. No part of this book may be reproduced, scanned, or distributed in any printed or electronic form without permission. Please do not participate in or encourage piracy of copyrighted materials in violation of the author's rights. Purchase only authorized editions.

Although every precaution has been taken to verify the accuracy of the information contained herein, the author and publisher assume no responsibility for any errors or omissions. No liability is assumed for damages that may result from the use of information contained.

My Girls Publishing Fort Worth, TX

Print ISBN: 978-0-9913947-6-0

eBook ISBN: 978-0-9913947-7-7

Also by Joe B Parr

The Victim
Stolen Innocence
Unseen Carnage

For all those who helped me along my journey. Thank you for providing me with a life changing experience.

Table of Contents

Introduction
Part One – First Things First
    1. Why write a book
    2. What kind of book should you write
    3. How to start writing
Part Two – Before You Start Writing
    4. Inspiration / Themes / Stories / Topics
    5. Research
    6. The building blocks
    7. Thoughts / Ideas
    8. Story Structure / Outlining
    9. Characters
Part Three – Hands On The Keyboard
    10. One Chapter at a Time
    11. Writing Mechanics
    12. Weathering the Storm
    13. Keeping the Flow Going
    14. It's all about the Senses
    15. Don't stop writing
Part Four – The End… Not Exactly
    16. After 'The End'
    17. Editing
    18. Publishing
    19. Formatting
    20. Sales and Marketing
Go Tell Your Story

JOE B. PARR

Introduction

"I've always wanted to write a book…"

Every author has heard this statement more times than they can remember. Whether at a book signing, a party or a family reunion, it is almost a guarantee that someone will say that before the day is over.

Few authors mind hearing it. In fact, most authors smile inside when they hear it because they can relate. At one point in time, they too, wanted to write a book.

Besides, most authors love what they do and they love talking about their books, their motivations and their process. Almost every author, published or not, novelist or academia, has made that same statement at some point in their lives.

The reality is that everyone has a story inside them or an interesting family history or knowledge that they feel the rest of the world should know. And they should be encouraged to pursue that story.

Think about all the conversations over the years that you've had with friends, family and coworkers. How many times have you heard someone tell a great story or speak knowledgeably on an interesting topic and you found yourself completely enthralled? How many times has that someone been you and one of your friends said, "you should write that down."

Your friends are right. You should. It's incredibly fun and rewarding.

Someone saying they've always wanted to write a book is almost always followed by the question – "How did you do it?"

That's the question that I hope this book will answer for you. My objective is to provide you with a step by step process to help get your story from your head to the page to your readers.

What I've tried to do in the following pages is explore that question in the context of my journey from average reader to avid reader to letter and journal writer to published author.

What I'm not trying to do is to teach you how to write. While I'll provide some tips along the way, I'm not a writing teacher and there are far more qualified resources available.

Since most of my experience is writing fictional novels, you may notice a slight leaning toward that type of writing when I talk about techniques and examples. If your desire is to write nonfiction, don't worry, almost all of the advice, tips and techniques apply to nonfiction as well. That is especially true for Section Four in this book. I will try to highlight along the way where there are differences.

It's been an amazing experience, one that I hope isn't over just yet. So sit back, get a glass of your favorite beverage and follow along with my journey. There will be times throughout the book where I may mention how long it takes or how much work is involved. But don't let the enormity of the task stop you from pursuing your dream. You have a story to tell, and the journey is absolutely worth the effort.

Hopefully, I can help you find your way. And maybe, just maybe, it will give you the confidence to embark on your own trip.

Who is Joe B Parr?

It might make sense to tell you who I am and why any of what I'm writing should matter to you.

Let's answer those questions in reverse order. Why should you listen to me?

Simply put. I've been there, done that. I am not a classically trained or formally educated author. I'm just a guy who wanted to tell stories and make a difference and thought he could do it by writing books. I was in your shoes just a few years ago and I scoured the internet, went to classes, joined writer's groups, watched interviews with authors, listened to podcasts and most importantly I asked every author I could find how they did it.

SHARE YOUR STORY

The result has been a journey that so far has resulted in three Mystery Suspense Crime novels published in Amazon Paperback, Kindle and Audiobook as well as the book you are currently reading.

My fictional novels are a series set in Fort Worth, TX featuring FWPD Homicide Detective Jake Hunter and his team. Each of the three novels focuses on a specific social issue.

- The Victim – Gang Violence
- Stolen Innocence – Human Trafficking
- Unseen Carnage – Drug Abuse

While I haven't made the New York Times Best Seller list yet, my books have been sold in seven different countries and all across the United States. They've afforded me the opportunity to do regular book signings and occasional guest appearances at book clubs. Based on the average Amazon rating of 4.8 out of 5 stars across the series, I'm also very pleased with the reader reception.

Since I figured out this process by leveraging a tremendous number of resources, it only makes sense that I ask for input from some of the very people who helped me in my journey. I've asked a handful of successful authors I know to provide quotes, comments, thoughts and suggestions throughout the book. I will provide more biographical information for each at the end of the book, but here's a quick introduction to my panel of expert authors.

Jeff Bacot, Literary Fiction - *On The Hole*
Susan Sheehey, Romantic Mystery – Multiple Titles
Kimberly Packard, Mystery Suspense - *Phoenix*
Kenneth Ingle, Science Fiction – Multiple Titles
Chris Crawford, Speculative Fiction - *The Tuning Station*
C. A. Szarek, Historical Fantasy Romance – Multiple Titles

There is nothing more satisfying than having a complete stranger tell you they've read your books and loved them. That feeling makes all the hours of dedication worth it. It's a feeling that everyone should get to experience and one that, with some work and patience, you can achieve.

I hope this book helps you get there.

Part One:
First Things First

Chapter 1:
Why write a book

There is so much to talk about before your hands ever touch the keyboard. I know from my personal experience, the step from non-writer to typing the first words of my first manuscript took years.

My journey truly started because of my job at the time. I was a business consultant. This meant two things; First, I had to write a lot for work. It had to be coherent, correct and compelling. After all, most of the time, I was trying to convince someone to spend millions of dollars or I was trying to help someone justify why they'd already spent millions of dollars. So, although I didn't know it at the time, I was honing my book writing skills.

Second, I traveled extensively, which meant I spent a ton of time by myself in airports, on airplanes, in hotel rooms and eating dinner alone. A truly glamorous lifestyle. I had to fill that time with something and reading books seemed to be a logical choice. I started with nonfiction, mostly biographies and business books. Later, at the urging of my wife, I read my first Michael Connelly novel. I was hooked before the airplane landed.

But even though I grew into an avid, almost rabid, reader, and I knew that I had the basic writing skills required to articulate a thought, I was still a very long way from embarking on the seemingly impossible task of writing a book.

Without getting too philosophical, there really is a fundamental question that you have to ask yourself before you even start thinking about writing anything longer than a letter, much less an actual book.

That question is 'why do you want to write a book at all'.

I don't mean that flippantly. Writing a book, fiction or nonfiction, is a hell of a lot of work. It will likely take you anywhere from several months to possibly several years to complete. Without having a very real reason to write it, the chances of finishing it are almost nonexistent.

Maybe you are one of these folks who were just born to write. It's like breathing to you. You've written since you were a child and writing a novel is just the next logical step.

If that's the case, I hope my practical steps will help you, and I look forward to reading your masterpiece.

If that's not the case, put some thought into your personal motivation and make sure it's going to be strong enough to carry you through.

Every person has their own reasons. My guess is that you probably have multiple reasons for wanting to take this leap. I'd bet that not all of them have truly surfaced.

Some potential reasons include:

Personal Challenge – You want to prove to yourself, or possibly someone else, that you can do it. That can be motivating, certainly for a while. But I'm more than happy to restrict my personal challenges to doing ten pushups. At least with that challenge, the time from start to failure is usually about a minute, not two years.

Emotional Catharsis – Writing can be great therapy and it certainly beats talking about your problems. Depending on the type of book you want to write, this could be a driver. If you have a moving, personal story that you're driven to share with the world, the healing aspect of putting it in writing can be powerful.

It can also be a wonderful way to get a message out to the world about your experience.

Creative Angst – You just feel the need to tell your story. This probably applies mostly to that group I mentioned earlier, the ones that were born to write. For those folks, it's almost more painful not to write.

SHARE YOUR STORY

Self-Education – It's said that if you really want someone to learn something, make them teach it. Writing has a similar effect. If you really want to learn about a topic, research and write a book on that topic. If you really want to learn how to write, jump in with both feet and write a book. By the time you finish that first manuscript, right before you throw it away, you will come to the realization that you know how to write.

Ego – You can't wait to sign your first autograph or read your first Five Star review. Both events are quite moving. There's no doubt that going to your own book signing, taking pictures with readers and hearing someone say wonderful things about your book are all really cool. But I'd be surprised if that motivation alone will get you through the next several months or years.

Legacy – You want your kids, grandkids and great-grandkids to remember you. After all, books last forever. While that may be a great motivator, I might suggest spending more time with them and taking lots of pictures.

Earn Money – The last, and probably worst, reason to write a book, is the expectation that you're going to make a lot of money. Sure, best sellers happen, blockbusters do exist. But the odds are ridiculously long.

Here are just a couple of statistics for you to digest. The last time I checked, Amazon had almost seven million book titles available for purchase. Just selling one book a day will usually rank you in the top one hundred thousand. That means that six million, nine hundred thousand titles are selling less than a book a day. Depending on your pricing, you will typically make anywhere from $1 to $3 per copy. I'll let you do the math.

Why do other authors write?

"I have no choice but to write. It's part of my DNA." – Kimberly Packard

"Because I have characters talking to me all the time, demanding I write their stories." – Susan Sheehey

"I can't imagine a world in which I didn't write." – C.A. Szarek

Those are all valid reasons. For me, it ultimately boiled down to a sprinkling of almost all those things plus a heavy dose of two others:

Message – While I do write fiction, in all of my published novels, I try to address a social issue and to convey a message. In *The Victim*, I discuss gang violence and prompt the reader to think about their preconceived notions of good guys and bad guys. In *Stolen Innocence*, I highlight the issue of human trafficking, it's impact on society, especially how it disproportionately affects poor and minority communities. My third novel, *Unseen Carnage*, tackles the topic of drugs, the War on Drugs and the impact these have on the community, the victims and law enforcement. In my upcoming novel, *Murder by Proxy*, I explore the world of computer hacking, cyber bullying and cyber manipulation.

If your life story includes a trauma you've experienced or a challenge you've overcome, there may be a lesson the readers can learn. You can share that message.

Make a Difference – I see my role as a novelist as more than just entertaining readers. I'm trying to make them think about topics they typically wouldn't. Hopefully, that prompts them to get involved and take some kind of action.

With this book, I'm also hopeful my experiences, lessons learned, and advice can help other potential authors to get their stories told.

For me, my goal of making a difference becomes my motivational driver to keep writing when otherwise I might give up.

What will keep you coming back to the keyboard night after night?

Chapter 2:
What kind of book to write

My guess is that if you're reading this book, you probably already have at least a vague idea of what kind of book you want to write. But I thought it was worth a quick review of the possibilities. After all, when I started writing fictional novels, I would have never guessed that somewhere down the road, I'd be writing this book.

Once you get the writing bug, there's no telling where it might lead you.

Up until the publishing of this book, all of my writing had been fictional novels. Specifically, I write in the Mystery / Suspense genre. My only real reason for choosing that genre was because that's what I liked to read. At the end of the day, you need to write whatever it is that gets you excited, even if that means creating you own genre.

Here are some quick thoughts on the various genres.

Fiction – The dictionary defines fiction as 'the class of literature comprising of works of imaginative narration'. In other words, stuff that you make up based solely on your imagination.

Within the broad brush of fiction, there are genres. Some of the most common include:

- Literary Fiction
- Mystery / Suspense
- Science Fiction
- Romance

Examples of fiction range from the Harry Potter series of novels by J. K. Rowling to *The Great Gatsby* F. Scott Fitzgerald and *The Da Vinci Code* by Dan Brown. The main purpose is entertainment.

Nonfiction – The dictionary defines nonfiction as 'the branch of literature comprising of works of narrative prose dealing with or offering opinions or conjectures upon facts and reality'. The thing I find most striking about that definition is that nonfiction doesn't have to be true. I think there is a common misconception that 'fiction is made up' and 'nonfiction is real'. That is just not the case. Nonfiction can be almost as imaginary as fiction as long as it is commenting on fact or reality.

Within the broad brush of nonfiction, there are genres. Some of the most common include:

- Biography / Autobiography / Memoir
- Educational / Self-Improvement
- Political
- Observational / Philosophical
- Business

Examples of nonfiction range from The Tipping Point by Malcolm Gladwell to Leadership by Rudy Giuliani and The Four Hour Work Week by Tim Ferriss. The main purpose is to inform.

In both cases, fiction or nonfiction, when the author dips into the other category and blurs the line a bit, it can really get good.

Fictional novels that address real live issues or events can be an amazing combination of entertainment and education. Novels such as *The Jungle* by Upton Sinclair where his story tells about the workplace conditions that brought about the union movement in America.

That is something I've attempted to do in all of my novels. Whether addressing gang violence, human trafficking or drug abuse, I try to have a theme built into the story that informs the reader.

Nonfiction authors can play this game too by telling about a real historical event with real live historical characters, but told in a storytelling format. After all, a story is so much more compelling than a narrative.

Whatever category and genre you decide to write, the age-old

SHARE YOUR STORY

advice rings true. Write what you know. If you're an historian, write nonfiction about history or possibly a fictional novel set in a specific time period. If you're the local Medical Examiner, write Mystery novels based on autopsies.

In either fiction or nonfiction, you need to bring something new and interesting to the table. Author Ryan Holiday said, "the worst mistake authors make is that they don't have anything to say". If you're writing nonfiction, establish an angle, a specific situation, a message or a viewpoint not expressed before. If you're writing fiction, bring a new setting, character type or twist to the genre.

The most important aspect of writing isn't the writing at all. It's the story. Poor sentence structure will be forgiven. A bad story won't.

Tell a good story. Tell your story.

Chapter 3:
How to start writing

Before you open up your laptop to begin your first book. Before you stare at a blank page, knowing that you have three hundred more to follow. If you are truly a novice to writing, might I suggest some baby steps?

How about you start by just writing? And by writing, I mean anything and everything. In the beginning, what you are writing isn't as important as the act of getting something down on paper. Getting used to crafting words into sentences and sentences into paragraphs. Getting used to transforming a thought running through your head into a series of statements that convey meaning.

"The secret to writing a novel is simple. You write! Chapter by chapter. Word by word. Until it's done." – Chris Crawford

"It's scientifically proven that you can't edit a blank page. Trust me. I've tried." – Kimberly Packard

"Everyone has an untold story that should be told." – Jeff Bacot

As I mentioned earlier, before I ever attempted a book, I had been writing for years at work. In addition to writing for work, I was a regular letter writer and I'd kept a journal for years. While you might not think that kind of writing is connected to writing a book, I'd strongly disagree. All writing types share common characteristics. In all, you are trying to communicate thoughts and ideas.

One of my first experiences outside of work, with writing something for public consumption was distinctly nonfiction – the annual

SHARE YOUR STORY

Parr Family Christmas Letter.

I know that may sound silly, but creatively summarizing all the escapades of the various family members without boring people to death is not an easy task. I've written a letter every year since 1999 and we typically mail out over 300 each year to friends and family. Some years are funny, some are serious, but each has a theme that is woven throughout the letter.

Interestingly enough, to a certain extent, I credit those letters with giving me the confidence to know that I could write in an entertaining and meaningful way. I had so many people respond with variations of 'we loved the Christmas letter' or 'you ought to be a writer' that I eventually took them seriously.

It was also my first experience with having a certain level of pressure to write well. Over the years, there were numerous friends and family that told me how much they looked forward to the letters. With that, there were more than a few years where I felt like a real writer with a real audience. Even if it was 'just friends and family'.

If you are planning to write personal life based nonfiction, you should be journaling every day. Not just to be collecting stories and thoughts, but to get used to writing seriously about your world, your views and your feelings. Even if it's just a journal, pouring your soul out on paper can make your heart beat a little heavier.

Keep in mind. Depending on the nonfiction style you're writing, that journal may actually end of being your first draft.

Once I decided I wanted to try my hand at writing a fictional novel, I created opportunities to practice. This came in two very specific ways. First, I'd try to remember and recreate my dreams on paper, as if they were scenes in a movie. That not only helped me with the technical craft of describing a scene in writing, it also helped me to think creatively as I would typically have to take fragments of dreams and fill them out into a scene.

The second thing I'd do was to just come up with random scenes and try to write them. A confrontation or fight scene. A romantic dinner conversation. I really focused on bringing in all aspects of the scene to try to make it as vivid as I could.

There was no pressure to be great since I never shared these writings with anyone else. I just, as objectively as I could, read, critiqued, edited and rewrote them until I got them to a point where I felt like they could have been plucked from a 'real' novel.

Being able to paint an accurate and compelling scene is equally applicable to nonfiction writers. Let's take an example. If you are writing a memoir about how you survived a car wreck, you have two choices. You can simply state that your car was hit from behind and fell down a cliff. Or you can paint the picture of the car wreck as if it was plucked from the pages of a novel with all the graphic descriptors about your heart racing, glass shattering and metal scraping. Which one do you think will be more compelling?

As a final suggestion on how to get started, and this one takes a tremendous amount of commitment, but it's how I started. Write a 'practice book'. That's right, a full blown, 200+ page book with characters, plot and dialog. If you know from the very beginning that you're not going to show it to anyone, there is no pressure. No writers block. It's just you and a bunch of terrible pages of writing that will be the best learning tool ever.

That's what I did. I took a bunch of people, places and things that I knew, jumbled them up, fictionalized the heck of them, and wrote a story. It took nine months but at the end of it, I had a 250-page, 55-chapter novel with multiple story lines that all tied together and came to a logical conclusion.

It was awful, but it was done. And by the time I'd finished, I'd made every possible mistake and had learned from each one. To this day, the only person who's read it other than me, is my wife. She gave me the ultimate compliment. She said, "it doesn't suck".

How could I not go on and write three more books with that kind of ringing endorsement?

Part Two:
Before you start writing

Chapter 4: Inspiration/Themes/Topics

Inspiration. The muse. Divine intervention. Whatever you want to call it. It's that force that stirs your emotions, sends that tingle through your stomach and maybe even makes the hair on your arms stand up.

It can hit like a bolt of lightning or it can hide like a lost set of keys.

But when you really think about it, inspiration is everywhere. Anything that creates a spark in your senses. That sight, sound, smell, touch or taste that can create a thought or an image in your mind.

The smell of the ocean might make you want to write a novel based in the islands.

The sight of a social injustice that spurs you to research the issue and write a nonfiction book on the topic.

The smell of motor oil and exhaust might inspire you to craft a character who races stock cars.

The sound of a blues song may get you interested in the origin of the Blues enough to write a book tracing the history of local artists.

You get the idea. The feel of soft sheets. The vista of a mountain range. The taste of BBQ. It can be anything that gets you going.

What inspires the authors from my panel?

"People and my interactions with them." – Jeff Bacot

"Everywhere and nowhere. For me, it's all subconscious. Ideas are just there." – C.A. Szarek

SHARE YOUR STORY

"My favorite 'idea in waiting' came to me in a dream. The main character talking to me." – Kimberly Packard

All of those conjure up images, thoughts and ideas. Those naturally flow into the creation of stories.

Stories are the natural extension of inspiration. Much like inspiration, stories are everywhere. Every person walking down the street has a story. Even the most boring of us have done something or seen something or experienced something interesting in their lifetime.

I think I've lived a pretty normal, not overly crazy life. But I've traveled a lot for work, so I've experienced cities, states and countries in a somewhat unique fashion. I also had one seriously off the charts week in Cozumel with one of my best friends that someday will work its way into a book. I may have to change some names to protect the guilty.

Keep in mind that the term interesting doesn't necessarily mean fun or enjoyable. Unfortunately, some people experience interesting misfortune or challenges in their lives. Not all stories are happy. Some of the most epic stories of our time revolve around people facing enormous challenges. The story often is about conquering those challenges. Sometimes the story is merely about the struggle against the odds.

If inspiration isn't jumping out at you through your senses and the stories you're seeing in your everyday life don't seem to warrant a few hundred pages, then you may have to dig a little deeper.

When trying to find a story that has meaning for you, think in terms of four areas:

- People you've known
- Places you've been
- Experiences you've had
- Things you've encountered

When was the last time you dug around in your attic or your closet and found something that reminded you of a story from your past? Maybe it was the ribbon you won at the elementary spelling bee or the program from a play in which you performed. It could be anything that sparks a memory. That memory, combined with the wisdom of hindsight, can be crafted into a story.

This same mindset can be used with people you've known such as former teachers and coaches, family members or coworkers. Places you've been for work or vacation almost always have a story attached to them. Maybe at the time, they didn't seem important, but now that some time has passed, and other events have occurred, their significance has grown. Ditto for any experience in your life.

The difference between nonfiction and fiction for these four areas is simply whether you are applying them specifically to your life and trying to craft a story about you or someone you know or whether you apply that same lens to one of the characters in your fictional novel.

Another approach I've used, especially for fiction, is to mix and match the backgrounds and stories of the people around you. That can be an effective way to come up with something totally new. For example, maybe you have a friend who is a singer-songwriter and another friend who is a police detective. If you combined those into a single character, what kind of crazy stories could you come up with for a detective who plays the bar scene at night? Could be fun.

Another avenue could be newspaper or magazine articles. You can take a component or a character type from the article, expand it into something totally unique.

David Lee Roth, the original lead singer for the band Van Halen, once spoke about how the band wrote songs. I'm paraphrasing, but he said, "They'd start playing someone else's song that they liked. Then they'd change one part, then another and another until the song was completely unrecognizable and was unique to their sound." I'm not sure how true that story is, but it certainly sounds like one way to get there.

When you really need to give yourself a kick in the pants, you can google 'writing challenges'. There are dozens of sites with multiple lists of various types of writing challenges that are fun and just might revive your muse.

I often like to work from a theme perspective. This leans a little toward the nonfiction world. Themes for me, are usually focused around what I want the reader to take away from the story. Do I want to raise awareness about an issue? Do I want to motivate the reader to

SHARE YOUR STORY

take action?

With a strong theme, the more I research, the more motivated I am to craft the story. With my second novel, *Stolen Innocence*, the theme was human trafficking. As the father of two daughters, the more I researched the issue, the more consumed I became with telling the story. Once I got moving on the manuscript, it almost wrote itself.

In nonfiction, it's more about a specific topic or theory that the author wants to communicate or prove. As discussed earlier, there are many different kinds of nonfiction, but most start with some form of thesis.

In academic nonfiction, proving that thesis through deep research, experimentation and reasoning, is the core reason for writing the book.

Many nonfiction books are derived from the author's own life experiences or observations. Much like fiction, the inspiration can be anywhere. Your terrible experience on an airplane may spark you to write about trends in airline service. Your dining experiences on your recent Mediterranean trip might motivate you to write a cook book.

Even with nonfiction, getting readers interested always comes back to telling a good story. The best nonfiction tells a story based in the same kinds of imagery that works in fiction. Put the reader in the story by invoking their senses.

Finding your inspiration, a moving story, a motivating theme or an interesting topic usually requires you to pay attention. Live in the moment and observe the world and the people around you. What are their challenges, their triumphs?

The story is there.

What have you experience recently that, with a little thought and research, could be turned into a book?

Chapter 5: Research

Regardless of the type of book you are writing, there will likely be components of the book that will require you to search for information. Even with the fluffiest of fiction, you need to have some level of accuracy in settings, props and actions.

This is where research comes into the picture. The term 'research' in the writing world can mean many different things to many different people.

If you are writing a scientific or academic based nonfiction book which is trying to prove a thesis, research may be defined in the scientific sense. This may include formal studies, lab experiments, statistical or scientific modeling. Your book may be the culmination of years of work.

Within that world, there are very strict standards and rules an author must follow in order for their work to be considered valid by their peers in that industry. There are complete textbooks written and devoted to the topic of scientific and academic research. I'm not an expert in that field and won't attempt to bluff my way through it.

If you are a scientist or professor wanting to write that type of book, I won't be able to help you on the topic of research. However, if you are a scientist or professor wanting to write a crime novel or a memoir, I think I can give you some direction.

Research for most writers is really about getting educated on a topic, location, industry, hobby or activity. If you are a crime novelist, you should know a little about guns. I learned that the hard way in my first novel. In the first published version, I made two very specific mistakes when talking about guns and ammunition.

The first mistake was that I misspelled the gun manufacturer, Beretta. The second mistake was making a statement about why someone would or wouldn't use hollow point bullets. I got it backwards.

Fortunately for me, a couple of my very early readers were gun aficionados and brought it to my attention before too many copies were in print. These were embarrassing mistakes that could have been avoided with just a little more homework on my part.

My point is that, even in fiction, readers expect you to be accurate in your descriptions of things, events, activities and places. All of my novels are set in and around the Fort Worth, TX area. Fortunately, I've spent most of my life in the area and know it extremely well.

Still, I like to bring in the history and flavor of the various neighborhoods around town. Since I'm not an expert in all aspects of all parts of the city, researching becomes a process of searching for unique cultural aspects of various sections of the city. These need to be accurate or I run the risk of offending local readers.

So, how do I approach research?

Fortunately, we live in the information age when you can find information on almost any topic within a few clicks. The following is a list of tools I've used routinely as sources of information.

- Internet
- Library
- Newspapers
- Periodicals
- Books
- Interviews
- Television
- Documentaries
- Podcasts
- Genealogy Sites
- Family Records

In some respects, there's almost too much information out

there. In fact, one of the challenges is sorting through everything you find and making sure the information you have found is accurate. I know it's hard to imagine something you find on the internet might not be true.

If it's an important fact and you don't have first-hand knowledge, I'd strongly suggest verifying the information from multiple sources. And at least one of those sources should be something more reputable than 'bobknowsitall.com'.

You usually don't have to chase down hard copies of books or documents. In today's world, most books, magazines and newspapers are digitized and can be found online.

Now that we've talked about where to find the information, the next question is when.

As I've mentioned, even though my novels are fiction, I like to base them around social themes and to include real statistics and data points that help add validity to the story.

For me, becoming as educated as I can about the topic before I start writing is critical. One of the side benefits of researching a social issue, is that it builds your inspiration and adds layers to your story.

In my novel, *Unseen Carnage,* the initial idea was to write a story about the devastating impact of the War on Drugs in low income and minority neighborhoods. I read several articles and books and watch documentaries on the topic.

As that process unfolded, I got more excited about the book. But I also realized that I was missing some components to the story. Those components included the negative impact that drugs have on the users and their families as well as how the constant battle of fighting drugs affects law enforcement personnel.

By the time I was through with researching the book, my perspective on the story I wanted to tell had changed dramatically.

If you're writing a personal story or memoir, you may think that research isn't necessary. After all, you lived the story. I get that. However, I'd still suggest double checking facts, locations, dates and names. Just because your crazy Uncle Bob told you something happened doesn't mean it's true.

SHARE YOUR STORY

Who knows. You may discover a whole new layer to your story once you do some digging.

Research is more than just chasing down facts and figures, it's about uncovering the whole story.

Chapter 6:
The building blocks

This is probably a good spot to make a point about the overall process. I've laid this book out in a linear fashion because, well, that's just the way a table of contents works. But it's important to understanding that almost any of these steps can happen in any order. And most happen continuously and in parallel throughout the process of writing your book.

As I mentioned in the previous chapter, the action of researching a topic can become inspirational and can dramatically change the story you originally set out to tell.

The further we get into the process of writing, the more you will find that each step along the way is an opportunity to revisit and refine the steps you've already taken. A word of warning. You will have to learn to control the impulse to rethink every decision. Otherwise, you will find yourself in a never-ending loop of indecision.

While it's great to improve on your story with additional information and layers, at some point, you must stop adding ingredients and let the soup simmer.

Now it's time to start getting a little tactical. You've been inspired. You've determined the type of book you want to write and have the basic idea for a story or a topic to be explored. There are stacks of research documents and artifacts laying all around your workspace.

How do we start the process of molding all of this information into something coherent enough to type on the page? Over the next three chapters, I will cover what I consider to be the most important tactical components of creating a book. That statement assumes that you have a good story, because that is the single indispensable ingredient.

There is a short list of tools that I use to get the story ready for writing. There is nothing fancy or impressive about them and for each, you can find multiple versions and formats used. You will probably end up creating your own version to suit your taste.

The tools are:
- Concept Notes
- Story Outline
- Character List
- Character Profile
- Character Relationship Map

What tools are used by other authors?

"Phrases Sell and The Phrase Finder." – Ken Ingle

"I recommend using Scrivener as a writing tool. It can be daunting at first but eventually, its features can make you far more productive." – Chris Crawford

"I have character sheets that I fill out for each main character." – Susan Sheehey

I've dedicated a short chapter for each of these, combining the three focused on characters into one chapter. And yes, technically speaking, you will have your hands on the keyboard and in some regards, you will be creating content that may end up in the first draft of your manuscript.

Chapter 7: Thoughts / Ideas

Finally, I get to type something. It's about time. Yes, it's time to key something into your computer and the good news is that you don't have to worry about if it's any good, how it reads, how it's formatted or if anyone will like it.

I call this my Concept Notes. I'm sure other authors call them different names. Some probably don't even have a name for it at all.

The basic idea is to do a mind dump on paper. All of your inspiration, your thoughts about themes, any ideas you've had about scenes or plot or characters or dialogue.

This process is needed for both fiction and nonfiction.

You need to get them into a document. I use MSWord simply because it's the only word processing tool I know how to use. You can use anything. Just start writing.

While I said you don't have to worry about structure, I do have a very loose structure that I use. I'll start with a couple of paragraphs that outline the overarching story. Think of it as your very first cut at the book's synopsis. Doesn't have to be good. I'd make sure that I include the overriding theme or topic if there is one.

From there, I'm going to break it out into several sections:

- Theme Points – If you have an overriding theme, what are the main points you're trying to get across to the reader?
- Overarching Message – If this is a memoir or a story designed to teach a lesson, you need to think about the

message or messages you want to convey.
- Research Points – Are there any specific statistics, data or historical facts you want to make sure are included?
- Potential Characters – If it's a series, you don't have to list the regulars. I'd only list new ones that are pertinent to the story.
- Story Setting – Same as above. If the series is always in the same city, there's no need to waste time.
- Potential Scenes – Stuff you've already pictured in your mind. Fill in as much detail as possible.
- Potential Dialogue – By this time, you've probably already had a few pithy lines pop into your head. Get them on paper.
- Potential Plot Twists or Points of Conflict – What have you already thought of for your characters to conquer?
- Questions to be Answered – This is usually a long section and usually just short bullet points. These are questions that you, as the writer, don't know the answers to yet.

Within these sections, Concept Notes are random, almost stream of consciousness. They're notes detailing anything and everything you can think of pertaining to the book.

For me, this process can take weeks as I continue to mull over the story and theme. At this point in the process, always having your laptop with you, or at the very least a notebook, is critical. Thoughts are going to pop in the middle of the night, when you're in the shower, at school, work or church. When they pop, you want to immediately get them into the document.

The idea is to just let your mind go free without worrying about form or if it makes any sense. All you're trying to do is ask the question, 'What if' and document all the possible answers.

After a few days, weeks or months, you will naturally start to run out of stuff to write down. By then, you will likely have anywhere from ten to thirty pages full of stuff.

At that point, you can put more organization to the notes. I do this by organizing each section a little more deeply. I might segregate the dialogue by character or the scenes by location.

For one of my novels, I created a high-level time line for the story arch.

Some benefits I experience while writing these notes include a much deeper understanding of what I'm trying to tell the audience as well as a much better idea of where the inflection points for the story might fall.

At the end of the day, this document becomes a garden of thoughts and ideas that you can continue to harvest throughout the process.

Chapter 8:
Story Structure / Outlining

We're getting so close to attacking that first blank screen, I can almost taste it. But hang with me for just a little longer.

I'm really not trying to drive you crazy with all this pre-work, but based on my experience, the more of this you do, the easier it will be to face that first page with confidence. Keep in mind, that most of these steps are overlapping each other quite a bit. In fact, even once you start writing, you will likely go back and forth between writing and updating your thoughts.

First, some not so original thoughts on story structure. I'm not breaking any new ground in this section. There are hundreds of books, articles and essays all across the internet that are written by people for more technically adept than me on this topic. While I haven't made it my life's mission to analyze these structures, I do think a high-level understanding is important. Therefore, I've reviewed several of them and will attempt to summarize now.

Once again, I can't stress enough that understanding the elements of a story and learning how to craft a good story are critical to writing a good book, regardless of whether it's fiction or nonfiction.

My guess is that you've at least heard of the concept of the Three Act Story. At the very basic level, almost all books, movies and plays are loosely structured around this idea. Aristotle is credited with the original thoughts and apparently based it around the audience's need for intermission.

The three acts are simply the beginning, the middle and the end. Let's look at each for a moment as well as their major subcomponents

The Beginning – Often referred to as Act One, this section of the novel focuses on establishing the protagonist as a character along with defining his environment. It also sets up where the book is going.

The subcomponents include:
- The Opening Scene – The objective is to draw the reader into the world of the protagonist and establish a baseline for the setting, the rules and the core character traits.
- The Inciting Event – This is an opportunity to make a change in the protagonist's world or to fix a problem. It establishes the conflict that is at the heart of the novel.
- The Act One Problem – This gives the protagonist a goal to accomplish and usually requires a decision. When he decides to act, it sets up Act Two because now he's set on a path that creates danger or conflict and pushes him outside his comfort zone.

The Middle – Act Two is all about the struggles, growth and learning the protagonist goes through in the process of solving the Act One Problem. This is the meat of the book. In a Mystery Suspense novel, this will include having the protagonist go down numerous blind allies and chase a few red herrings.

This is much like what happens in real life. If you are writing a memoir, that probably means that you faced some challenges.

The subcomponents include:
- The Choice – Transitioning from the Act One Problem is the protagonist's choice on whether and how to deal with the problem. It often ends in failure because of a core character flaw that will eventually have to be overcome.
- The Reversal – This is usually where something unexpected happens that disrupts the protagonist's view of the world. It raises the stakes and creates personal consequences. It could reveal a secret or require some

level of sacrifice.
- The Disaster – As the name implies, this is where everything goes wrong. The big plan fails. The stakes are raised again, and the protagonists finally sees the truth of his flaws. This is the dark moment when the hero almost gives up, but finally summons the strength to carry on.

The End – Act Three is the conclusion of the journey and is focused on how the protagonist finally faces his antagonist in the ultimate battle. He'll use everything he's collected along the way to win. This brings everything to a final climax and then resolution.

The subcomponents include:
- The Plan – As the protagonist has summoned his last ounce of resolve, he uses everything he's learned to come up with a clever plan for the ultimate victory. The plan may get altered in the Climax, but the protagonist believes it going in.
- The Climax – The final showdown where the protagonist faces his enemy. Often the stakes get raised again during the action making the last battle even more important.
- The Wrap Up – The hero saves the damsel in distress and they all ride off into the sunset and live happily ever after. This is also where the reader gets resolution and understands there was a point to the novel all along. This is their final payoff.

That sums up the basic concept of the classic story structure. The good news is that there are no rules. You can follow a specific structure or not. Most authors use aspects of structure as guide posts and move in and out of the lines as necessary to tell their story.

The important idea of structure is to establish your characters and environment and then challenge your characters to grow, change and evolve. All while ramping up the conflict and tension until you give your characters and the reader a way to resolve the story in a satisfactory way. Notice, I didn't say provide a happy ending. Satisfying and happy aren't necessarily the same thing. Sometimes happy just isn't in the cards.

Now that we've talked a little about structure, let's talk about a tool that could help you define your story within a structure. That tool is outlining, or maybe not...

In the fiction world, there are two types of writers. Those that outline and those that don't. Those that outline are usually referred to as Plotters. Those that don't are often call Pantsers. Get it... They write by the seat of their pants. We writers are a witty bunch.

If you are truly a Pantser, feel free to skip to the next chapter and move onto the next step. However, even a Pantser may want to at least think about jotting down some basic direction on where they want their first few chapters to go.

A few thoughts from our panel:

"I don't plan, I just sit down and write." – C.A. Szarek

"I'm a pantser. I don't like fleshing out a story when I start. I like making it up as I go." – Jeff Bacot

"I've discovered that without at least a basic outline to follow, I write myself into corners." – Susan Sheehey

In reality, on the fictional front, I don't know anyone who outlines the entire novel before starting to write. I'm not sure that's possible. Even if it's possible, I'm not sure it's productive since I feel certain it would change dramatically before you got through the first third of the book.

Most writers I know are hybrids. They will outline a few chapters, enough to get a good start. Then they will periodically, every few chapters, revisit the outline to extend it out a few chapters. I personally like to have a rolling ten-chapter outline.

All I'm really trying to do at this stage, is to get a basic order of events. I need enough information in the outline so that as I start to write a chapter, I can come up with a specific list of actions that need to take place in that chapter.

Within the outline, for each chapter, I'm going to note the point of view (through whose eyes is the story being told). I'm also going to note the physical location, time of day, day of the week and month of the year.

SHARE YOUR STORY

Each of these points helps to keep the story moving forward and keeps me from making really basic mistakes. You don't need your editor asking how can it be Monday on page ten when it was Tuesday on page nine. It's also a little confusing if in Chapter Nine you talk about it being December and in Chapter Ten, you describe someone as sweating in the summer heat.

I know those sound like mistakes you'd never make, but I only mention them because I've been there and done that. It's just a whole lot easier to take thirty seconds to refer to your outline before you start writing a chapter. It will get your mind wrapped around the scene setting.

The last thing I'll do for each chapter is to write out a paragraph or two detailing what's going to happen in that chapter. I don't kill myself with details. All I'm trying to do is get the basic flow and start running that flow in my head.

Regarding outlines, to this point, I've been focused on how outlines are used in fiction. In nonfiction, it's very different. I know with this book, my outline did cover the entire book and within each chapter, I had a lengthy list of bullet points that needed to be addressed in the chapter.

Because there are so many different types of nonfiction, ranging from academic dissertation style to personal memoir, you may have to experiment a bit to find out how much you need to outline.

The overriding purpose of the outline is to give you the guideposts you will need to craft each chapter and to have the chapters flow in a way that tell a compelling story. As with everything else we've discussed, the outline is a fluid document that will be updated throughout the life of the book.

Chapter 9: Characters

I don't think it's an overstatement to say that every great book or movie or play has at least one great character. I know I said that the most important aspect of writing a good book is to have a great story. I'll stand by that statement, but I'll add to it that most great stories have at their core, a great character whose personal qualities fuel that story.

How do other authors see characters?

"Characters drive story and conflict the best. Flesh out the characters forward and backward, and you'll find the plot and conflict create themselves." – Susan Sheehey

"Sometimes the characters do / say things that shock me. I've learned to listen to them and be the navigator." – C.A. Szarek

"I love a good storyline, but without these fantastic characters, it would be boring." – Kimberly Packard

Understanding that the word great in this instance could take many forms. Good guys, bad guys, crazy people, wonderful people. Any can be a great character if you give them the right qualities.

The logical question then is, how do you write a great character? There are entire books dedicated to this topic, but I think the answer is all around you. When you look at the people in your orbit, who are the ones that you find most interesting? Who are the ones that either attract you or repulse you? Who are the ones that you can't seem to ignore?

In my opinion, the one common denominator with good

characters is that they are innately human. They have a definable personality. They have good qualities and bad qualities, strengths and flaws and human emotions.

Just like the rest of us, most great characters have a look and identifiable quirks or habits. They have dreams and desires and fears. It's usually the combination of those dreams, desires and fears that create the internal and external conflicts that can be the heart of a really good story.

In nonfiction, you may not have the latitude to create a character. The characters may already be defined for you, as in the case of a biography, autobiography or memoir. But it's up to you to define and expose all those characteristics to which the reader can relate.

You can fill a biography full of interesting facts, dates and details, but unless you get beneath the surface to make the reader understand that the rock star or politician is just as emotionally messed up as they are, you won't be able to get their attention.

Whether you're writing fiction or nonfiction, one way to get to the essence of writing great characters is to do some serious self-examination. By that, I mean really analyze yourself to understand what are your dreams and desires? What stands in your way of achieving them? What scares the hell out of you?

Now, follow that same process with the characters you're creating. After all, you have complete control. You can make them as messed up as you want. In fiction, the more messed up, the better.

I think most fictional writers subconsciously, sometimes on purpose, write parts of themselves into their characters. It's an easy way to make them real. I may have gone out of my way to not write a single character that resembles me, but I know that there are bits and pieces of me scattered throughout the characters in my books.

Don't worry that you don't have each character completely mapped out in advance. Just like you, they are going to evolve, change and grow as you write about them. In fact, leaving a little space can give you the flexibility to build layers onto your character down the road.

You do need to at least start with a baseline and make sure there's enough substance to give you something to mold.

That brings me to the three tools I use when I start working with characters. Those are the Character List, Character Profile and Character Relationship Map.

The Character List is exactly what it sounds like. It's a listing of every character in the book. It's a list that grows as you write the book and should include any character that is named or described. This should include the barista, the bartender and the auto mechanic.

The reason I include everyone is that if you don't, you're apt to make a mistake such as describing the same bartender at two different points in the story, but calling him two different names. Besides, you never know when you may need that bartender to become a bigger part of the story and you're going to need some basic information on him.

The information on the list is pretty basic.

- Name
- Nickname
- Role, Title
- Very basic description
- Any distinctive characteristics

Keep it high level. The main use for the Character List is just to keep track of who's who and to make sure that, if you're going to call out this character's blue eyes, make sure he didn't have brown eyes three chapters ago.

This list will be ever growing as your book expands, but having a handful of characters defined before starting chapter one is important.

The Character Profile is the next tool in the arsenal for character development. There are dozens of formats available on the internet. All of them cover many of the same components.

They basically walk you through a series of questions, the answers to which will define your character. What are her physical characteristics? Eye color? Hair color and style? Body type? Etc. What are their personality traits? Talkative or quiet? Happy or sad? Etc.

A character profile will touch on:

- Physical Description
- Attitudes

SHARE YOUR STORY

- Job
- Skills
- Gender
- Interests
- History
- Relationships
- Quirks
- Flaws
- Habits
- Beliefs
- Speech
- Ambitions
- Fears
- Pet Peeves

The list can go on and on. You get the point. You are building your character from the ground up. I think it's critically important to think about these questions for each of your main characters. I would caution you a bit to be careful not to over define your characters to the point that they become difficult to write.

I like these profile forms, but I use them sparingly. I give my characters enough back story and details to make them developed, but I keep enough open space for the story to reveal other aspects. The other issue with profiles is that they can become time sinks. You can spend hours, days or weeks filling out forms and thinking about every little detail for every character. By the time you get finished, you may be too exhausted to write.

The last tool I use for characters is the Character Relationship Map. This is the Business Consultant coming out in me. Consultants have never met a PowerPoint slide or Visio diagram they didn't like. There's nothing quite like a flow chart to get the blood pumping.

Since I write Mystery / Suspense, the plots can get a little involved. Trying to keep track of who's married to whom, who works where and who's Bob's cousin can be mind numbing. And in the Mystery genre, the entire story can hinge on the fact that Fred was

Tim's half-brother by the mother they never met.

It's critical that the author keeps all the relationships very crisp in their mind.

A Character Relationship Map is simply a visual representation of who is related to whom and how. You can use a software program like Visio, a chalk board, a dry erase board or even a cork board with paper and stick pins.

It's really just a bunch of boxes and circles depicting characters that are then connected by lines and arrows with notes outlining the relationship.

You might have Bob who is Fred's son, but he's also Tommy's boss and Susie's boyfriend. In that case, Bob's box or circle would be connected to boxes for Fred, Tommy and Susie. For each, the relationship would be noted as well.

The Character Relationship Map is a completely optional tool, but it can be very helpful to help you visualize the connection points in a story. If you are a visual person or if you have a lot of characters, or if the relationships between those characters are complex, this might help.

Whether you use any or all the tools I've mentioned for creating your characters, the cardinal rules are to keep them authentic and interesting. The reader must care about them in order to want to read about them.

So, we're done with the pre-work. Those are the major steps I take and the tools I use before I sit down to start writing. Sometimes, that process takes days or weeks. Sometimes, it's months or years.

However long it takes, I have consistently found that the better I do these steps, the easier it will be to actually write.

Part Three:
Hands on the keyboard

Chapter 10:
One Chapter at a Time

Okay, there it is. It's staring at you. Don't blink. Don't pull your hands back. It can sense fear. Don't let it win.

There's nothing quite as scary as a blank sheet of paper. Especially when you know there are another three hundred behind it. But if you've done all your homework, you're ready to win this battle.

Just keep in mind, it's one chapter at a time. Really, it's one word at a time. The trick is to get something on paper and keep going.

How do other authors face that blank page?

"There's only one response. Sit down and write." – Ken Ingle

"I write the scenes as they occur to me. I generally don't write in order, which drives some people crazy." – C.A. Szarek

"I usually put in all caps where I need this chapter to end." – Kimberly Packard

"I try to start and finish a chapter in one day. Otherwise, I don't sleep." – Jeff Bacot

If you've followed the steps laid out in the previous chapters, you're not only inspired to write but you also know why you're writing. You have a good sense of the story you want to tell and how the book is going to flow.

All the major components are in place; story, setting, plot and core characters. You've also outlined at least the first few chapters, maybe more.

So, how do you transition from pre-work to writing. It can be intimidating. That's why I break it down by chapter and focus on writing one at a time.

I view each chapter as its own story. Kind of a mini-book. Just like a book, there must be a reason for writing the chapter in the first place. Some basic questions should be asked and answered.

- What needs to happen in this chapter?
- Where is the chapter set?
- From whose point of view is the chapter told?
- How does the chapter move the book forward?

Once you've answered those questions, you need to think in terms of the story within the chapter. That story, like all stories, needs to have a beginning, a middle and an end.

In fiction especially, but applicable to all types of writing, the beginning of the chapter, or for that matter, the book, is critical. After all, it's your one opportunity to capture a reader's attention. For that reason, it's often referred to as 'the opening hook'.

Beyond getting the reader's attention, you have to make them want to read the rest of the chapter or the book. The first sentence, or paragraph, in the book is how many readers determine if they are going to keep the page open and read or close the book and put it down.

Each chapter is much the same. You want to start in a way that engages the reader immediately and makes them want to keep reading that chapter.

There are several ways to grab the reader. My novels make heavy use of dialog to push the story forward, so I will often start a chapter with a character speaking. That forces the reader to scramble a bit for context, which engages them immediately.

If a chapter starts off with, "I thought I told you never to come back here again", the readers mind must move quickly to determine who is speaking, to whom are they speaking, where are they and why did he say those words.

Of course, as a writer, you will answer all those questions in the next few pages.

Another alternative is to start with an action statement. It works much the same way as dialog. The line, "A gunshot shattered the quiet night", forces the reader into the same process. Who shot whom? Where are they? Is someone dead, or hurt?

Early in my writing career, I was given some great advice from my editor and fellow author, Susan Sheehey. She told me to always start a chapter as far into the scene as possible. You can always backtrack and provide context and description.

In other words, if the main point of the chapter is that someone has snuck into someone else's room to shoot them, instead of starting the chapter describing how they crept down the hall and quietly opened the door, start the chapter with them raising the gun and squeezing the trigger.

It's the 'oh my' effect that grabs the reader and sucks them into the chapter.

Nonfiction can work much the same way. Many memoirs and personal stories are written in story telling style, so the same mechanisms used to grab attention in fiction translate well to memoirs. Other nonfiction can use a bold declaration or a provocative question to kick off a chapter.

Scenery descriptions can sometimes work, but they will usually have to be directly tied to the previous chapter, and specifically tied to some sort of cliff hanger in that chapter. For instance, if the last chapter ended with the hero commandeering a plane, but left the reader hanging as to where he was going, then starting the next chapter describing waves lapping up on the shore gives the reader a level of resolution that will likely keep them engaged.

However you do it, the objective is to make sure the reader doesn't put the book down at least until this chapter is done.

The middle of the chapter, much like the middle of the book, is all about moving one or more of the plot lines forward or provide the reader with new information to build out one or more of the characters.

Even though the reader has already committed to reading the chapter, the job of keeping their attention isn't over. With that in mind, pacing is everything.

As with the beginning, action and dialogue can play important roles with driving the motion forward. It is usually a balancing act between providing scenery, setting and context with action, movement and dialogue.

The objective of the final paragraph or sentence in a chapter is the same as in the beginning. Readers tend to use the end of a chapter as a place to stop reading for the night. As an author, there's nothing better than getting someone to stay up late. The best compliment I've ever gotten is that someone was tired because they stayed up all night reading so they could find out what happened.

With that in mind, 'the ending hook' really has two key objectives. First, you want to wrap up the chapter in a way that is satisfying to the reader. Make sure there is enough of a payoff that the reader feels like they didn't waste their time. Second, you want to set the stage for the next chapter and the rest of the book.

This can be done in much the same way as beginning the chapter. You can leave the reading hanging with a pithy piece of dialog or stop the chapter just as the car is plunging off the cliff.

In the nonfiction realm, chapters are often started and ended with questions or statements which promise to get answered over the next few pages.

Whether fiction or nonfiction, as a writer, you want the reader to think, "okay, just one more chapter before I go to bed".

Chapter 11: Writing mechanics

The mechanics of writing a chapter are really straight forward. Your basic objective is to take what's in your outline, or if you're a Pantser, in your head and get it on to paper. The trick is that you are most likely starting with a list of actions or events that need to take place in order to move the story along, and your job now is to turn that list into a story.

Let's walk through the first three steps in the process and then we'll look at an example from one of my books.

Step 1 – Start with your notes from your outline or the notes in your head. This is likely in paragraph format and is probably pretty loose.

Step 2 – Determine the characters involved in the scene or scenes, the setting and point of view.

Step 3 – Create a list of bullet points of actions or events that need to take place in this chapter.

Following is an example. Chapter 27 from Stolen Innocence.

Outline Paragraph: *Go to interview the surgeon. Claims to have never heard of JLJ and doesn't know anything about human trafficking. Go to Sledge Properties and talk with HR. Claim neither man is still employed and that both were just basic handyman help. Start to get media interest. Sprayberry getting nervous. Trying to keep it quiet. Get autopsy report linking the ballistics to the same gun as JLJ. Killer is so bold not to even bother changing guns.*

SHARE YOUR STORY

As you can see, this is very unstructured. There's not a lot of detail considering this chapter turned out to be over 2,800 words.

Because this was a pivotal chapter where several different people were involved in separate places, it required the chapter to be broken up into divided sections. This gave me the freedom to have a different point of view and a different setting for each of those sections.

This is a useful device when you need to amp up the urgency in the action and you have events that are taking place simultaneously. You can bounce from one scene to another and back in the same chapter. They are part of the same chapter for the very reason that they are occurring at the same time.

So, in this case, Step Two, my decision on characters, settings and point of view turned out to be multiple.

Step Three – The bullet point list.

- *Go to interview the surgeon.*
- *Get suspicious when they learn where he lives*
- *Claims to have never heard of JLJ*
- *Doesn't know anything about human trafficking*
- *Go to Sledge Properties and talk with HR.*
- *Claims neither man is still employed*
- *Both were just basic handyman help.*
- *Start to get media interest.*
- *Sprayberry getting nervous.*
- *Trying to keep it quiet.*
- *Get autopsy report linking the ballistics to the same gun as JLJ.*
- *Killer is so bold not to even bother changing guns.*

As you can see, it's really just a bullet point version of the information in your outline. Usually, I'll add bullet points around bits of dialogue or setting.

I will create this bullet point list in the body of my manuscript under the heading for that chapter. I do this for two reasons.

First, it gets something on the page. I'm no longer looking at a blank sheet of paper. The intimidation factor drops immediately. You can't have writer's block if you've already started writing.

Second, as you write above the list on the page, the list moves down with you and you can delete each bullet point as you complete them.

Sometimes you'll find that, at the end of the chapter, you still have bullet points left. At that point, you either need to figure out how to go back into the chapter and plug them in, or decide where they should go. Maybe they need to be in a future chapter or maybe the story has shifted, and they don't belong at all.

This is a good point to bring up the reality that your story will change as you write. You may get to a chapter and as you're moving through the process of getting it on the page, you realize that your direction needs to shift. Either you realize that the character, whose point of view is being presented, would do something different than you drafted in your outline or you just have a creative moment and come up with a new twist or direction.

When that happens, it can be great. It can also mean some rewriting and maybe even throwing away some parts you've already written. As painful as that might be, if the new direction has gotten you excited, it will probably get your readers excited as well. Don't be afraid to let your characters tell you how the story should go.

One of the reasons I will only outline five to ten chapters at a time is that the story will often shift as I write a chapter. When it does, I will go back to my outline and translate those adjustments into new chapters.

Once you've taken your outline paragraph, determined your characters, setting and point of view and keyed in your bullet point list, now it's time to start creating your story within the chapter. The good news is that you are not looking at a blank sheet, you're looking at your list of bullets.

Your first decision is how to kick the chapter off in a way that grabs the reader's attention and makes them want to read the chapter. As we discussed previously, dialogue or action are very good ways to accomplish this.

In our example of Chapter 27 in Stolen Innocence, here is the opening paragraph.

"You didn't get to me in time." The sound of the girl's voice made him turn to the right. When he saw her, he was drawn to her eyes. They were hazel, hypnotic, the pupils were wide and her expression grim. *"You knew where I was. What took you so long?"*

I started the chapter off with dialogue, but I also threw in a twist in that I started it off with a dream sequence. The main character is dreaming about the victims of the crime.

In this case, I'm purposely disorienting the reader. They won't know it's a dream until a few paragraphs further. They also have no idea who's speaking or to whom they are speaking.

The intended effect is that they will be curious enough to read at least the first page of the chapter. By that time, they are emotionally committed and will likely read the rest of the chapter.

Now that you have them committed to reading the chapter, your job is to walk them through the list of actions and events in a way that keeps their interest high. As discussed before, this requires a mixture of action, dialogue and movement. It's all about pacing.

In this case, because it's a long chapter, I've broken it up into several shorter components. Each of those components are a unique set of characters, action and setting. They're bite sized chunks that move back and forth quickly. The effect is the buildup of momentum.

The final step is to bring the chapter to a close in a satisfying way for the reader, but in a way, that makes them wonder what's next.

Going back to our example of Chapter 27 in Stolen Innocence, here's how I closed out the chapter.

"Hey, you ready to roll?" Barkley's voice brought him back.
"Yeah, we've got work to do."

Here we have the two main characters wrapping up what just happened but letting the reader know there's more to come. Not the greatest hook I've ever written, but in this case, the chapter was a lot to bite off at one time, so the reader probably needed to catch his breathe.

Once you've got the chapter written, print it out and read it from beginning to end making notes in the margin about parts that need to be added, deleted or changed.

Rinse and repeat.

When you think you've got it, have someone else read it. This isn't so much about grammar, periods and commas. It's more about pacing and movement. Ask them the big picture questions: Did it make you want to turn the page? Are you interested in what happens next?

At this point in the drafting, you just want to make sure that you are pushing the story forward and keeping the reader's interest. There will be plenty of time to edit for word choice, grammar and punctuation.

So, those are the major steps I take when writing each chapter. Sometimes a chapter flows out in a few hours. Sometimes, it can take days or weeks.

Following these steps not only makes writing the chapter easier, it also ensures that the completed draft advances the story in a satisfying way.

At least, satisfying enough for the first draft. We'll cover editing and rewrites in a future chapter.

Chapter 12:
Weathering the storm

Have you ever driven on a long stretch of highway in the deserts of New Mexico, Arizona or West Texas? There are times when the road in front of you is so long that it just disappears into the horizon. If it's in the heat of the summer, even that horizon is blurred by heat waves.

Writing a book is much like taking a journey. With every journey I've taken in life, there were stretches that felt like that West Texas highway at 3pm on a hot August afternoon.

Some motivating thoughts from other authors.

"There is someone out there who needs your story. As much as you need to tell it, they need to read it." – Kimberly Packard

"Seriously, don't give up. If you want it, get it." – C.A. Szarek

Regardless of the greatness of your story or the level of your passion, there will be a few times, most likely several, along the way where you'll be facing that heat wave obscured horizon. When you do, what will be the driving force that gets you to take that next step or write that next chapter?

Is your 'why' strong enough to not only get through the hard times, but also to just dedicate the necessary time on a daily, weekly, monthly basis?

If you plan to be a full-time writer, then BE a full-time writer. That means approaching it like a job. The novelist John Sandford told the audience at a book signing I attended that he writes a minimum of 1,500 words a day. That's every day. Seven days a week. That's in addition to his traveling, speaking, interviews and other promotional events.

For most writers, getting 1,500 usable words written is hours, sometimes days, worth of effort. There have been many times in my writing career that I would have killed to get 1,500 words in a week.

Most first-time authors are likely to be trying their hand part time. Even so, the time commitment can be daunting. As a part-time novelist, if you can commit ten hours a week, realistically it's going to take you anywhere from nine months to two years to finish your first full manuscript. From there, assuming the core content is worthy, it will take another three to six months to edit, rewrite, proof and format your manuscript into an actual book.

So, optimistically, that's one year. Realistically it's two to three years. Are you mentally prepared for that marathon? Are the people around you mentally prepared for that marathon?

Having a strong, or at the very least, a tolerant support system is critical. Your spouse, your children, your friends, fellow authors, maybe even your boss should be considered when you launch your plan.

What I've found is that, even though I might schedule my 'writing' time to be late in the evening or early in the morning, or in the case of my first two books, when I was on an airplane or in an airport, that doesn't mean that I wasn't constantly thinking about plot lines, characters and scenes. That constant mental process can be incredibly distracting and tends to turn you into an absent-minded participant in the rest of your life.

It's bad enough if you're daydreaming at some six-year old's birthday party, but getting busted for not listening to your wife for the fifth time in one evening, well, that can get pretty dicey. Worse yet, drifting off in the middle of a meeting at work.

In order to avoid divorce or disownment from your family members, I'd suggest making them a part of the process. Use them as sounding boards for plot ideas. Let them help you name characters. My wife is the person who reads the second draft of my manuscript and I'll often ask her to read individual chapters along the way.

SHARE YOUR STORY

I would highly recommend using your friends and fellow authors wherever possible as readers. Joining a writers group is one of the best things you can do. You'll get tons of free advice, critiques and support from people who have already been in your shoes and successfully moved forward. All the coaching I got from the Greater Fort Worth Writers group was invaluable.

As for the boss and drifting off in meetings, learn to compartmentalize. If you really can't keep yourself from thinking about your book while at work, at least try to do it at lunch or on breaks.

Writing a book is a big task that can become all-consuming if you let it. Leverage your schedule, your discipline and your support system to get to the horizon.

Chapter 13:
Keeping the flow going

One of the challenges with any long form writing, fiction or nonfiction, is trying to figure out how to balance pacing with substance and how to make sure you've created enough twists and turns to make it interesting for the reader. Twists and turns in the nonfiction world could just be unanswered questions.

We've all experienced hearing someone, who doesn't like talking, tell their life story. They usually manage to sum up fifty years of life in four or five sentences. *I grew up in Texas. Got in trouble with the law. Spent some time in jail. Got out. Started a business. Now I'm rich.*

Well, that certainly hits the main points and gets you from the beginning to the end. But it manages to leave some details out. And it's those details that make a story worth reading.

We've also all experienced the opposite. The guy at the party who can talk for an hour straight about his trip to the grocery store yesterday. He certainly provides plenty of detail, but really, did we need to know that the checkout clerk once played little league soccer? I didn't think so.

Clearly, there's a balance to be found when writing. Whether you're trying to figure out how much to write or if you're just trying to figure out where the story should go, there are a few questions you can ask yourself along the way that may help you keep the flow going.

Following are some of my go to questions.

What if? - I'd like to say that I'm the originator of that prompt, but I stole it from Steven Canell of TV fame. That doesn't lessen its power. It's a simple question to ask yourself anytime you might be stuck. Even if you're not stuck, it's a great question to liven up a fictional scene.

- What if he said this?
- What if she did that?
- What if the car broke down?
- What if the gun wouldn't work?

In the nonfiction world, the questions might be:

- What if we explore the background of a particular topic?
- What if we went deeper on the meaning of this or that?

You can go on for days with 'what if' questions, and every one of them has the potential to take the story in a new direction or give your character something to resolve.

Is this believable? - While I know that certain genres of fiction have no basis in reality and therefore, nothing in the book is truly 'believable', even in complete fantasy, there is a structure in place that governs the action. After all, if space aliens showed up in the middle of a Harry Potter novel, most readers would find that more than a bit odd. Whereas, when Dobby the House Elf shows up, it's perfectly in context.

In the Mystery / Suspense genre, believability is crucial. Any action or set of circumstances, at some point, has to be explained in a way that the reader will buy as believable.

In nonfiction, not only does it have to be believable, it must be provable at least through reasoning, if not through the presentation of factual evidence.

What is the character thinking and why? - Part of believability and good character development is routinely getting in the heads of your characters. A character's actions are driven by their thoughts. You don't always have to explain what they're thinking, but you, as the writer, need to understand what they're thinking if you want their actions to make sense.

This is equally important in nonfiction. If it's a memoir, you may be the character. In many cases, exploring what you were thinking is the whole point of the story.

Part of pacing the story is the mixture of action, dialogue and thoughts. Where are good points to show what the character is thinking?

What you may also find is that when you ask yourself this question, the answer you get may present a revelation in the story. The realization that a certain character would think a certain way when confronted with a situation may make you realize that there's a new direction required for the story.

What is the character feeling? – This works much the same way as the character's thoughts, only more visceral. Sometimes a character can do something that doesn't make sense because of an emotional reaction or a feeling they're having. The action may not make sense on the surface, unless you show the feeling or emotion that is driving that action. Once you do, the action becomes believable.

Why should the reader care? – With this question, you get to put yourself in the reader's mind. Making the reader care, of course, should be paramount in everything you do, but unless you remind yourself on a regular basis, it's very easy to get so wrapped up in plots, subplots and descriptions, that you forget why the reader is holding the book in the first place.

Where is the story going next? – This goes back to the outline and always keeping in mind where you're driving the chapter. You know how you need the scene to resolve and you know, at least at a high level, what's going to happen in the next chapter. So, reminding yourself of those points is like finding breadcrumbs that lead you back home.

There are many more questions you can ask yourself along the way to keep the words flowing onto the page. All the basics of a good story – who, what, where, when and why. Those can all be applied to any character, any action or any scene. These are the questions that are bouncing around in the reader's mind and ultimately, if you want a satisfied reader, you'll figure out a creative way to answer them.

Chapter 14:
It's all about the Senses

Some of the greatest prose ever written is descriptive in nature. Using words to transport the reader from his recliner to a mountain range in South America or a beach in Australia can be magical. Painting a scene in a magical way is all about engaging the senses.

Incorporating multiple senses as you describe a scene is critical in connecting with a broad group of readers. Every reader thinks differently and reacts to different stimuli so only describing what a character sees runs the risk of leaving a large chunk of readers unsatisfied.

Just as there are visual learners, auditory learners and tactile learners, readers fall into the same categories. Where one reader is going to get excited when a writer paints a picture of snowcapped mountains, another will get turned on by the description of the sound the wind makes as it whips through the peaks and a third reader may get goosebumps when the author describes the briskness of the frigid air.

I'll often write a chapter with minimal descriptors and then come back after I've completed it to really focus on describing the scene. Much like we discussed in the earlier chapter about keeping the flow going, it's all about the questions you ask.

- What is a character seeing?
- What are they hearing?
- What are they smelling?

- What are they tasting?
- What are they feeling physically?

It's one thing to describe what a barn looks like, but you don't really understand a barn without the sweet, pungent odor of manure, the wet, musky scent of hay or the dry, stale smell of dust.

Describing a bar is fine, but to feel that bar, you need to hear the sounds of the music, the thump of the bass, the din of conversation and clacking of pool balls.

Even in nonfiction, I think the senses are incredibly important. If you are writing a story about men in prison. What does a cell smell like in the heat of the summer? How menacing are the sounds of the cellblock in the middle of the night as doors clang, voices mumble and convicts snore?

That covers the five basic senses as most people define them. But there's more to this concept. No, I'm not going to suggest there are more senses. What I will suggest is that, in the same bucket as senses, you can throw in thoughts, feelings, expectations, fears and premonitions.

For each one of those, the approach is similar only you really need to take it one step further. Not only do you need to ask the question, "What are they feeling?", you need to ask the follow up questions, "How is it manifesting?", and "What is it impacting?".

Someone may be feeling scared. Okay, that's great, but saying that 'his heart is pounding, and his hands were shaking' is better. Going to the next step to say that, 'it took him three tries to load the magazine into his gun', adds a consequence to his feeling.

Whether you're talking about the five basic senses or the additions that I described, the idea is to use whatever it takes to pull the reader into the scene. Done well, the reader won't be able to put the book down.

Chapter 15:
Don't stop writing

Everyone's heard the old saying, "How do you eat an elephant? One bite at a time." Writing a novel follows the same logic. If you let yourself think about the 300 blank pages in front of you, you'll be paralyzed. So don't.

Write one page at a time, one paragraph at a time or even one sentence at a time. What is the next thing that needs to be written to push the story or the concept forward? It's that simple.

That, of course, is easier said than done.

In order to be able to do that, you're going to have to take different approaches to see what works best for you. And you'll probably have to change those approaches a few times throughout the life of the book.

I've gone from scheduling specific times each day to write to setting a specific amount of time each day to write to just writing when the muse hits me. Each approach has worked at different times.

A marathoner approaches mile one much differently than they approach mile twenty-six.

For me, most of the time, just making sure I'm writing something every day works well. I don't try to force it. If I'm stuck on one book, I'll switch and see if I can progress on a different book. If that doesn't work, I'll write in my journal for a while.

What I have found is that the more you write, the more you will write. It builds on itself. I've heard it expressed many different ways, but there's a basic concept that you just need to write two crappy pages a day. Two turns into five which turns into ten, and out of those ten, you may have three or four that are usable. But it starts with the first two.

The other thing to remember is that no one but you is going to read the first draft. So it doesn't really matter how bad it is. Once you've finished that first draft, your story is written. From there, it's a question of pulling that story out of all those words that make up that first draft.

Part Four:
The End – Not Exactly

Chapter 16:
After 'The End'

If you've followed the steps in the previous chapters and worked relentlessly for several months, you now have a finished draft. First, pat yourself on the back. Congratulations on completing a full manuscript. You've just accomplished something that 99% of the world's population will never achieve. Allow yourself a few moments to feel great.

That's the good news. At the risk of raining on your parade, you're about halfway to where you want to be. Now you have to turn that draft into a real book. Let's talk about how you get there.

The question is, 'What happens after The End?'.

The answer, unfortunately, is 'a lot'.

I like to think about the post first draft phase in four major steps

- Editing and Proofreading
- Publishing
- Formatting, Artwork and Finalization
- Sales and Marketing

Within in each of those steps, there are multiple options, tasks and activities. So, let's jump in.

Chapter 17: Editing

Has anyone ever told you that your baby is ugly? Well, get ready because it's coming. Fortunately, the first person to tell you that will likely be the person in the mirror.

I've mentioned a few times throughout the book that you shouldn't worry about being perfect with each sentence or paragraph as you write, because no one other than you will ever read that first draft. That's very true. But now it's time for YOU to read it.

This can be very difficult for several reasons.

First, you just spent months, maybe years getting it finished. In your mind, you've already written, read, updated, changed and fixed almost every page in this book a few hundred times.

That may very well be true, but printing off the entire manuscript, sitting down and actually reading it from start to finish is a very different experience. It can be mind numbing and eye opening all at the same time.

Second, because it's very hard to be truly objective about your own work. After all, it's your baby and you've sweat blood over this thing. Sometimes we are blind to the flaws because we are so invested.

There are two schools of thought on this first read. Some will tell to do a pure read all the way through first, with no self-editing or markups. Others will tell you to markup and edit as you go. This is really a personal preference. I personally find it very hard not to edit something when I read it if it sounds terrible. And trust me, there will be sentences and paragraphs and maybe even chapters that you will read and wonder what kind of idiot wrote it.

If you are truly objective, it can be a very humbling experience. But as my daughter likes to say, humility is one of my best qualities.

However you decide to approach it, you really have to put on the hat of the reader. There are a series of questions that you need to ask yourself repeatedly throughout the process.

- Do I feel compelled to read the next page?
- Am I interested?
- Am I being entertained or educated or both?
- Does it flow?
- Does it make sense?
- Is it believable?
- Do I feel like I'm experiencing the story?

That's just a few. I'm sure you can come up with several more. You may notice that there are a few that are missing.

- Are there typos?
- Is everything spelled correctly?
- Is that proper punctuation?

On my first read, while I will correct those things if they jump out at me, I'm really not focused on them. My paramount concern is determining if the story is good and if I've told the story in a way that will engage the reader.

Trust me, that narrow focus will provide you with plenty of opportunities to edit, change and revise. The manuscript will likely be a sea of red ink by the time you're finished with that first pass.

Now comes the painful task of rewriting several hundred pages. The good news is that what comes out of that first rewrite will be light years better than that first draft. And the even better news is that no one ever had to see that terrible mess that was the 'first draft'.

There's a fine line between believing in your product and being delusional. In order to get as far as you've gotten, somewhere down deep you had to believe that you were capable. The importance of believing in your capabilities and in the product you've produced is about to be tested.

SHARE YOUR STORY

It's time to determine if the product is really good and not just your imagination. That means you need to get other opinions.

There are a couple of ways to do this and my suggestion is to pursue both avenues in parallel.

First, find someone you trust, whose opinion you respect and who reads enough to know good from bad, and ask them to read the full manuscript. This should be someone who can be tactfully, yet brutally honest with you and someone from whom you can accept constructive criticism.

In my case, that's my wife. She reads multiple books per week and likes Mystery Suspense novels. She knows good from bad, isn't afraid to tell me the truth and I respect her opinion.

Just like when you read your first draft, you should have this person focus on the same big picture questions. You're still trying to determine the quality of the story, how well it flows, and does it make you want to turn the page. As with your first read, if they notice typos and such, that's fine, but it isn't the objective.

In parallel to that full manuscript read, I'd suggest breaking up the manuscript into individual chapters and having multiple readers read one or two chapters each. It is best for these readers to have some level of experience in writing. Fellow authors are great for this exercise.

If you're not already a member of a writer's group or community, you need to find one to join. Being around other authors will not only motivate you to write more, it will help you to become a better writer.

Don't be offended when these reading requests come back with a sea of red ink on them. You want honest feedback. As with all critiques, you as the author have the final say on whether you choose to incorporate the suggestions or not.

Once you've collected all your feedback, it's a bit of a slog to wade through them all and determine what to keep and what not to keep. Be very mindful of how you incorporate the changes. Make sure that you are keeping the integrity of the story intact. The one danger is in accepting too many suggestions from too many different sources and in the process, destroying the continuity of the story.

Slog through, choose the suggestions to use, and get through the next rewrite.

Once you complete, at the very least you will need to do another full read on your own just to make sure you haven't broken anything.

It's time to talk about professional editing. If you're being published through a traditional, big named publishing house, professional editing is likely to be provided through them. If you are being published through an independent or if you are self-published, you will likely need to take care of this yourself.

Let's talk about the different types of editing:

- **Story Editing** – A professional Story Editor provides a detailed critique of the story, content and flow. Much like what you've asked your friends and fellow writers to do in the first two pre-read cycles. As before, the professional Story Editor is not necessarily looking for typos, spelling, grammar or specific wording. They will tell you if you have gaps in your story but won't necessarily tell that you need to change the wording on sentence 2 in paragraph 3 on page 12. The difference between this round and the first is that word, 'professional'. Your friends are great, but they don't want to hurt your feelings. That's really not a concern for the professional.
- **Copy Editing** – A professional Copy Editor provides a detail read to point out wording issues, phrasing issues, typos, spelling, etc. They will point out grammatical problems, run on sentences, the use of weak language. It's really all about tightening up the writing and getting rid of a lot of the filler. Don't be surprise when, after this process, your word count drops significantly.
- **Proofreading** – A Proofreader is really only looking for true errors such as missing words, misspelled words, etc. This is the final step before you transition from a manuscript format to a book format.

SHARE YOUR STORY

You have a lot of ways to approach the editing process. You can take each of these three steps as completely independent activities and move through them sequentially, doing a full rewrite in between each. Or you can combine them by doing Story and Copy editing together or Copy editing and Proofreading together. Or having the same person do all three at once. I don't recommend that final option. It's asking too much for one person to pull off in a single pass.

I personally try to combine Story and Copy editing in the same step. I'm lucky enough to have found an editor who has a talent for both and can juggle the two functions in a single pass. It's a good thing she has plenty of red ink.

However you combine and however many cycles you go through, after each will be another complete rewrite. If you are keeping count, we're now somewhere between three and five rewrites. As laborious as that seems, it's also kind of exciting because with each one, you can see the book getting better.

By the time you make your final pass with a Proofreader, you are very close.

The final step in the editing process will take place after you've formatted your manuscript into a proof copy of the actual book. That final step is Beta Readers.

- **Beta Readers** – We're back to friends and family or, if you already have a fanbase, you can reach out to some of your regular readers. You'll ask several of them to do a full read and provide comments. All you're really looking for from a Beta Reader is, 'do they like it'? This is your one last chance to make changes before you hit the big 'done' button.

All the various forms of pre-reading and editing take a tremendous amount of time. Because of that, you are asking friends, family and fellow authors to invest hours on your behalf. For basic reads with comments, asking this as a favor is probably fine. However, when it comes to real editing, I'm a firm believer in paying a professional.

Professional editing is usually done on a 'per word' or 'per page' fee structure and can really run the gamut on price. It can go from a few hundred dollars to a few thousand dollars for a full manuscript.

Editors can be found all over the internet via a google search. I would caution you, however, to really scrutinize someone before you send them your manuscript or cut them a check. What are their real credentials? Can they provide references? Do they have a history of editing the type of book you've written?

Following are some links to editors found on the internet. This is not an endorsement, merely a sample from a google search.

http://www.jenfitzgerald.blogspot.com/
http://ashleycase.com/
http://bevharrosproofreading.weebly.com/
http://www.bookeditorcoach.com/index.htm
http://cedarsky.net/
http://theeyesforediting.com/
http://www.everything-indie.com/
http://www.lastdraftediting.com/index.html
http://www.rachelstarrthomson.com/
http://rhondaedits.com/
http://www.victoryediting.com/services.html

Whenever possible, I'd strongly suggest using someone you know or someone who has been recommended by someone you trust. Except for actually writing the book, this is the most important step in the process to publishing a quality book.

I'm incredibly lucky to have found a fellow author, whose own writing is fantastic, but who also has the ability to do top shelf Story and Copy editing. Because we know each well, what she charges me is well below market. If you find someone like this, treat them right.

Unless you find yourself in my fortunate situation, the old adage that you get what you pay for often rings true here. Editing is demanding work and it takes a very specific skill set. Just because you can write doesn't mean you can critique or edit. In fact, most authors are terrible at it because they have a hard time breaking away from

SHARE YOUR STORY

their own personal style.

Whatever path you choose, do your homework and don't cut corners. You'll be happy with the results of a professionally edited manuscript.

Chapter 18: Publishing

Over the past decade, the world of publishing has been completely turned upside down. Not very long ago, there was really only one option if you wanted to publish a book. It didn't matter whether you were writing nonfiction or fiction and it didn't matter what genre. Publishing meant finding a traditional publishing house who was willing to publish, print, market and distribute your book.

The explosion of the internet, new software along with high tech printing and distribution technology has opened up the world of publishing to just about anyone who has something to write. That, of course, is both good and bad.

The good side is that the opportunity to get your work published, distributed and read is available literally to anyone. That is also the bad news. While it provides any writer with a platform and gives readers more choices than their minds can comprehend, there is absolutely no quality control on content. I have read some self published books that were so terrible I couldn't force myself to read past the first chapter.

While the various options we'll discuss have varying degrees of control on format and presentation, at the end of the day, if you are intent on publishing horribly written prose or worse, hate filled rhetoric, there is a path for getting trash on the market. It brings a whole new meaning to 'let the buyer beware'.

There are several different options and variations, but currently there are three major avenues for publishing. They are Traditional Publishing, Self Publishing and Hybrid / Independent Publishing.

What publishing path have other authors taken?

"I have ten books (science fiction) traditionally published and three books (mystery) self published." – Ken Ingle

"I was indie published but I'm transitioning to self publishing because I want to have more control." – Susan Sheehey

"I was with a small press at first but subsequently left them and started self publishing." – C.A. Szarek

Let's talk a little about the differences and the advantages and disadvantages of each.

Traditional Publishing – Traditional publishing has been the dominant business model throughout the history of the industry. It involves multiple gate keepers in the process and is controlled by a relatively small number of large publishing houses - Organizations such as HarperCollins and Simon & Schuster.

The process, while simple in theory, is very difficult to maneuver successfully in real life. An author first needs to convince a literary agent that they, their idea for a book, or their already completed manuscript, are worthy of being 'represented'. This usually involves writing query letters, drafting and presenting book proposals and providing portions or all of your manuscript for review.

Most authors never get past the first step. I've personally know several very talented authors who have presented in some fashion to dozens of literary agents with the only result being enough rejection letters to wallpaper a gymnasium. In many cases, your query letter is often screened by an assistant before it ever makes it in front of an agent.

If you are lucky enough to get the attention of a literary agent and they want to represent you, now the process starts all over again with your literary agent 'pitching' your book or book idea to publishing houses. The process is once again an uphill battle and one that usually means getting past a series of screeners within the publishing house before getting to a real decision maker. Based on the books I've read over the years, clearly taste is subjective.

Once you get a publishing house to want to publish your work, you are usually paid an advance on royalties and provided a contract where the publishing company takes ownership of the print license.

The author is still completely on their own for writing the book. Some publishing companies may provide editing. The publisher manages and controls the publishing and distribution process from there forward.

Advantages:
- Advance on royalties
- Media coverage
- Emotional high from 'being published'

Disadvantages:
- Odds of getting published are extremely long
- Time and emotional investment
- You lose ownership of your book
- No control over content or art
- Limited financial upside (lower royalty percentage)

The reality is that unless you are a known public figure, a celebrity or in some other way, have an established following who the publishing house is confident will buy your book, your chances of making it through the process are slim.

When you do make it through, you are still on the hook for doing almost all the marketing. You also may find your product being changed in ways that aren't appealing to you.

Still, there are some reasons to pursue this path.
- If you need the advance money
- If you need main stream media attention

Also, there is a level of prestige that comes with being traditionally published that, at least for now, self publishing doesn't quite match.

Self Publishing – As the name indicates, the author manages the publishing, printing and distribution process themselves or contracts out the various components. The author retains ownership of all aspects of the book and controls the entire process. You answer to only yourself with no deadlines and no creative oversight.

Sounds like fun, doesn't it? Before you start dancing, understand that when I say the author manages everything, what I really mean is that they 'do' everything. Unless you have unlimited funding, the chances of you contracting out many of the tasks are slim. That means hours of mundane activities such as formatting the internal text as well as learning to use new software tools so that you can create, or at the very least format the book cover.

You have to be your own boss which means creating your own schedule and plan for getting everything done. We'll talk more about marketing but you're either going to have to design bookmarks, posters, book displays, banners and websites or you're going to have to hire and manage someone to do it all.

All that stuff can really get in the way of writing. But, if you're a do it yourself kind of person, it can be very gratifying.

Advantages:
- Full ownership of everything
- Total control of everything:
    - Creativity
    - Marketing
    - Deadlines
- Move at your own pace
- Higher potential royalties

Disadvantages:
- It's a lot of work
- A lot of potential rework as you learn
- Time consuming
- If you do everything yourself, quality may suffer
- If you hire professionals, it can be expensive

If you decide to go the Self Published route, my number one piece of advice is to focus first and foremost on the content. What you write, how it flows and the story it tells trumps everything else. Most people will forgive the occasional formatting error or typo. They won't forgive bad content.

With that said, the beauty and curse of self-publishing is that you must do everything yourself (or hire someone to do it). When it comes to potential costs, it really breaks down into five areas. In each case, you can spend as little or as much as you want.

- Legal
- Editing
- Formatting
- Cover Art
- Marketing

Hybrid / Independent Publishing – I realize I'm mixing terminology in a way that might not be perfect. I'm trying to create a catch all bucket for all the variations that fall somewhere between Traditional Publishing and Self Publishing.

This mainly includes either using a small, regional or niche publishing house in a mostly traditional way or using a company who offers publishing services and who may or may not retain any level of ownership rights.

There are as many different versions of Independent and Hybrid Publishing as there are colors of paint. The main idea is that the writer and the publisher craft a unique agreement where they split or share the tasks, activities, ownership and revenue.

Advantages:
- You can get help in areas where you lack expertise
- Shared control

Disadvantages:
- Can be painful to navigate
- Self Publishing is probably easier
- Time consuming

Whichever path you choose to pursue, don't assume that anyone is going to do anything for you without getting something in return. They are either going to want some level of ownership of the final product or they're going to want to get paid for their efforts. It is a business after all.

SHARE YOUR STORY

More Details on Self Publishing

As Self Publishing continues to grow as a percentage of the number of titles published, I want to spend some time defining in more detail exactly how to go through that process. Besides, if you're going down the path of Traditional Publishing, it's not a bad idea to understand what's going on behind the scenes.

Let's start off on the legal side of things. The first thing you'll want to do with your completed manuscript is to get a copyright. This is a very easy on line process. You can simply google US Copyright. At the time of this writing, the website addresses for the official sites were: https://www.copyright.gov/ or https://eco.copyright.gov/. The second one is specific to Electronic Copyrights.

Through either site, you can register your work and pay a $35 fee and you will receive an official copyright for your work.

To my knowledge, I've never had anyone try to steal my work and since I'm not an attorney, I'm not sure how much true protection a copyright provides, but the peace of mind is worth the small fee. Plus, the copyright office actually sends you a certificate, which is pretty cool.

The next legal item is absolutely required. Getting an ISBN number for each version of your book is needed if you want to be able to sell it through any normal merchandiser. ISBN stands for International Standard Book Number. It is unique to your book and to each edition and variation of your book. It's very simply a way for retailers to identify your book to buy and sell. It's directly related to the unique barcode that will be printed on the cover.

Each version of your book will need a different ISBN. This includes hard cover, paper back and ebook.

You do have options on how to obtain an ISBN for your book. If you are using an organization such as Kindle Direct Publishing, CreateSpace, Lulu or Xlibris, you can choose to have them acquire the ISBN for your book. It's usually easier and cheaper, however that ISBN will only be good for the books published through them and they retain the rights to that ISBN.

The alternative is to purchase a block of ISBN numbers for your own that can then be used and controlled by you for whatever formats you decide to publish. Doing this allows you to use a single ISBN for all paper back versions of your book regardless of whether they are sold on Amazon, Barnes and Noble or in a book store.

It does cost more to do it this way, but you retain control. You can buy blocks of numbers through Bowker International. At the time of this writing, the costs are:

- $250 for 10 ISBN
- $575 for 100 ISBN
- $1,000 for 1000 ISBN

I chose to go this route and bought a block of 10 numbers. For each of my books, I've used one number for the eBook and one number for the paperback. I've published four books and have used up eight of my ten numbers. I'm well on my way to completing book five which will use up my last two numbers. When I'm ready for book number six, I'll buy another batch.

I like having complete control and knowing that I'm not beholden to any specific printer or retailer.

The benefit of both the Copyright and the ISBN is that once you're registered as the owner of a particular book, as long as you keep your registration information current, anyone looking for information on that book will be able to find you. This can be important if you actually want to sell books.

One thing to note, specific to Amazon Kindle, even if you have your own ISBN, they will still assign their unique ASIN or Amazon Standard Identification Number. That's their internal tracking number, it's free and it's automatically done.

To buy a block of ISBNs, go to:
http://www.isbn.org/ (US)
http://www.isbn.nielsenbook.co.uk/controller.php?page=121 (UK)

SHARE YOUR STORY

Self Publishing Formats and Channels

While there are variations within each format and channel, there are really four broad types.
- Hard Cover Print
- Paperback Print
- eBook (Electronic)
- Audio

For each of these formats, there are dozens of organizations available to help you get your product produced. Ultimately, most of them make their money off services they sell you or off the distribution of your product through their channel. In the case of Hard Cover or Paperback, they will also generate revenue for the print service.

Each organization provides its own set of tools, templates and services. I will cover the processes for the organizations I used, but understand that you have a ton of options. I chose my path for two main reasons. I wanted to maintain as much control as possible and I wanted to spend as little as possible.

For me, it was a very cool learning process, even though there were more than a few times when I wanted to throw my laptop through the window. In the end, I felt like the quality of the product was professional and the process worked well.

Hard Cover / Paperback – I'm a bit old school, so when someone talks about a book to me, I think of a real book I can hold in my hand and turn pages. There's just something about a real book that will never be replaced by eBooks.

With that in mind, I started my process focused on publishing in paperback format. I did not choose to publish in hard cover. For hard cover, you will have additional decisions to make and formats to review and the cost will be more, but the process is essentially the same.

For paperback, I chose to work with a company named CreateSpace. They are a subsidiary of Amazon, which has some advantages, and they are one of the leaders in self publishing. They make most of their revenue through printing and distribution. While they do offer some services such as formatting and cover design, they are really focused on the author who is self-sufficient.

As mentioned previously, you can google self publishing and find dozens of companies available to help. Just be aware that there are very few services these companies offer that you can't do on your own with a little effort.

The first step is to set up a user account on the CreateSpace website. The site is very user friendly and this process is easy. Once you have an account, you will create a project for your book.

When those basics are completed, it's time to make some of the core format decisions. These include book size and paper type. Maybe there's some magic to what book size you choose. If there is, I was never able to find anyone who knew. I just looked around at the people I knew and based my decision on my observation.

I chose 6 x 9 and a slightly off white paper stock.

Based on this decision, I was able to download a template from CreateSpace. The beauty of this template is that it already sets all your margins and offsets them correctly to accommodate for left and right pages.

While we'll cover formatting in a little more detail shortly, essentially you are going to cut and paste all of your content into the template. That will result in you now knowing how many pages there will be in your book.

Going forward, for future books, once I had the template, I did all my writing directly in the template so that when I hit 'the end', the book was already formatted. What a huge timesaver.

Now that you have the number of pages, you can download the template for your cover art. Again, we will talk more about cover design and art in a future chapter, but the important piece to know now is that the template will give you what you need to align the front cover, spine and back cover appropriately so that when they print the book, you won't have overlap.

It's critical to note two things. First, if the number of pages change through the editing and proofreading process, you will have to download a new cover template and adjust accordingly. Second, even with the template and software, getting your cover art exactly how you want it, can be very challenging.

The overarching process is straight forward and is presented in a step by step fashion on the CreateSpace website. Once you've got your book completely formatted and you have your cover design ready, you will go to the project you set up for your book and walk through the step by step.

The steps include filling in the following:

Title information - This includes answering several basic questions about the book. What's the title? Is there a subtitle? Who's the author? Etc. Most of the answers you will know off the top of your head. For those you don't, the site has easy to use links that will explain the question and why they are asking. I knew almost nothing about books or publishing when I went through this the first time and while it can seem a bit intimidating, most of it is very much common sense.

ISBN – You'll need to either choose to use the CreateSpace ISBN or provide your own. This was previously discussed. I provided my own.

Interior – Here's where you'll make your final decisions on paper stock, margins and size. Again, no magic, just personal preference. Keep in mind that before the process is done, you will get to see a proof copy of your book and you can change any of the formatting decisions at that point. This is the step where you will upload your manuscript in the MSWord Template format. Kind of a cool moment when you hit that button.

Cover – Same as with the interior, you will make decisions about glossy or matte finish and you will upload the pdf version of your cover design. One thing to note. This is one place CreateSpace steps in and forces a level of quality control. They will review your artwork for clarity and fit. This is so that the images don't overlap or come out fuzzy. They will not review it for content such as spelling or vulgarity. That's up to you.

File Review – Now that you've uploaded your interior file and your cover file, you will submit for review. This is usually a twenty four hour process. The CreateSpace team will send you an email with any issues they found. Again, not reviewing content, purely fit and format.

At this stage, you can review page by page on line. You also have the opportunity to buy proof copies. This is where CreateSpace will print a production quality book and ship it to you for your review.

This will be the first time you get to hold a book in your hand with your name on the front. Talk about a thrill. Take a moment to really appreciate what you've accomplished. Take some pictures. Kiss your spouse. Hug your kids. This is a big deal.

Don't be disappointed if it's not perfect. That's the whole point. This is an opportunity for you to go page by page and look for indention errors, typos, spacing problems. You'll also get to see and feel the cover. Do you like all the decisions you made? If not, go back through the process, change them and order another proof. You can do this as many times as it takes. The proofs cost about $5 each plus shipping.

At this stage, I know you're anxious to get done and go have your book release party, but take a breath and make sure you don't shortcut here. The world really does judge a book by its cover, and its formatting, and the number of typos. Make sure you get it right. It may take a few tries. I know I had a stack of bad proof copies for my first book. By my third, I think I nailed it on the first try.

Once you get it just right and you're happy with the proof copy that you're holding in your hand, go back to your project and approve your proof. All that means is that it's ready for printing when you officially release your book.

Now, there are a few more steps:

Channels – CreateSpace offers several different channels of distribution. Their main channel is through Amazon, but you get to determine whether you want it distributed in just the US or globally. They also offer several different channels of expanded distribution. Some of these may have a cost associated with them, but all of that is explained. It's a series of questions and check boxes.

You will also have the option of distributing exclusively through Amazon. When I first published, I chose not to go exclusively with Amazon. I was sure that I was going to sell a ton of books through the Barnes and Noble website and I didn't want to be boxed in to a single channel. I ultimately changed that decision and went exclusively with

SHARE YOUR STORY

Amazon. There are several factors to consider, not the least of which is the headache of maintaining multiple formats.

Pricing – You will need to determine your pricing model. CreateSpace provides a lot of information and suggestions. They also provide you with cost and royalty models for each pricing model you run. At the end of the day, you will have to do some market research by looking at bookstores and online for similar books and similar genres to help you determine the price you want to charge.

My two pieces of advice. First, do not think that you'll sell more if it's cheaper. I don't believe that to be the case. Most readers aren't going to make a book decision based on a price difference of a dollar or two. Second, if you are going to err, err on the high side. You can always reduce your price. Raising it isn't quite as easy. Also, keep in mind that you can always run promotions and specials where you can reduce the price temporarily.

Once you've made all your distribution and pricing decisions, you are ready to push the button. Go ahead. You're about to have your book published on Amazon. The process takes a few days, but you will get to see your book with its cover and synopsis on Amazon and you'll be able to direct your friends, family and fans to the site, so they can buy your book. You can also buy as many copies as you'd like directly from CreateSpace at the author's price. Congratulations. You are published. This would be a wonderful time to have a book release party where you'll get to sign your first autograph.

eBook (Kindle, Nook) – As part of the CreateSpace paperback publishing process, they offer to convert your book into Kindle format. I did not take that option. I wanted to control the process, so I decided to go directly to Kindle Direct Publishing for my Kindle format. At the time, I also went to Nook Press and published on the Barnes and Noble Nook eBook format. Due to lack of sales, I have since dropped that format and gone exclusively with Amazon.

One of the advantages of using CreateSpace for your paperback and Kindle Direct for your eBook is that they are both Amazon owned companies. While they don't share specific templates and tools, they do seem to share a mindset and an overall process.

Because of that, the steps you will go through for publishing an eBook on Kindle Direct Publishing are almost exactly the same as the steps you went through for your paperback. The differences you will encounter are really the differences required by the format itself.

Just like CreateSpace, KDP provides free templates and guidelines for both internal format and cover design. Yes, you still need a cover for an eBook. They will use that as the graphics for your book when it's on Amazon.

Some things that are different:
- The size and type of font for an eBook is different than a paperback. This is just for ease of reading which is different on paper versus a screen.
- Your cover design will only need a front cover. No spine or back cover is required.
- Pricing and royalties are different, but as with CreateSpace, KDP provides all the models and guidance.
- Proofing for an eBook is exclusively online. There's no need or advantage to printing a copy.
- Similarly to CreateSpace, there are some advantages to going exclusively with Kindle. In this case, those include having the book offered for free as part of the Kindle Unlimited program and being made available to Amazon Prime members to read.

As with your paperback, take the time to really review the entire manuscript page by page to make sure there are no formatting errors. The good news is that these errors are quickly and easily fixed, but if a reader buys and downloads a version with issues, you will likely receive a bad reader review. I'll talk more about reader reviews in the Sales and Marketing chapter, but just know, they are very important.

Once you have 'published' your Kindle format, contact Amazon through you KDP dashboard and ask them to link the print and Kindle versions together. This ensures that when someone searches for the book, they will see it's available in multiple formats.

For me, since I went through the paperback process first and because that process actually produces something you can physically hold in your hand, the Kindle process was a bit anticlimactic. It was still pretty cool the first time someone told me I was on their Kindle.

Audiobook – This will be the first point where you will be tempted to skip because you might think making an audiobook is too hard or too expensive. Don't. It's neither of those things and going through the process was one of the coolest parts of the publishing journey.

As with the other channels, there are dozens of companies out there who can produce and distribute your audiobook. Call me predictable, but I went with a company named ACX. They are, once again, an Amazon owned company. Amazon may be the evil empire, but they know what they're doing, and they make it very easy.

Much like CreateSpace and Kindle Direct, ACX has a step by step process to follow once you create your user account. This process is very different than the other two.

Some new steps and decisions:

On Air Talent – The first real decision you must make is, will you do the recording yourself or will you use a professional. Unless you have all the appropriate recording equipment, are really comfortable reading into a microphone and have a lot of free time to record and rerecord, using a professional is probably your best option.

Even if you have a golden voice and all the toys, you will likely still need a producer to take your raw recordings, clean them up and get them packaged for distribution.

This was a no brainer for me, and is for most people. I chose to have a professional do the recording. Yes, there is a cost for this, but let's cover that in a moment. It's not prohibitive.

Contract Type – The next decision you must make is, what kind of contractual arrangement you'll want to make with your producer and your talent. Note that while you can contract those roles separately, I saw absolutely no value in doing so since almost all the readers have the capabilities to produce as well.

There are two options on the contractual front. The first is to find the reader / producer and negotiate a one-time fee. Depending on who you hire, this can be several thousand dollars. For even a fairly unknown, it can be expensive. After all, reading, recording, polishing and packaging three hundred pages of a book takes a lot of time.

The second option is to split the royalties and ownership of the final product. ACX pays a standard total royalty of forty percent. On a twenty dollar audiobook, that's eight dollars. If you split that fifty-fifty, you and the producer will each get four dollars for every copy sold. Your investment is all the hours it took you to write the book. Their investment is all the hours it will take for them to record the book.

I chose the second option for all my books and had the same producer do them all. While neither of us have gotten rich, I think we'd both say it was worth the effort.

Along the way, I've made note of some of the very cool moments you will experience on your journey. I thought it was exciting to hold my first proof copy. It was also neat to see your book for sale on Amazon. But nothing prepared me for the emotional reaction I had the first time I heard my book read by a professional. It took my breath away. It was as if my words had come to life. The memory makes me smile as I'm writing this sentence.

Choosing The Talent – Now that you've gotten the legal stuff out of the way, the process really begins. You will submit a chapter of your book for 'auditions'. You can provide as much direction as you want. You can indicate you want a male or female, old or young, rough or smooth, animated or calm, etc. You get to be the Casting Director as various readers will submit their audition recordings to you for your review.

Just like an audition for a movie, you will listen to the recordings and decide which one fits the book best. It can be a tough decision. After all, these folks are pros. They're all very good. Usually it comes down to feel.

Recording The Book - Once you've selected a reader, you can work directly with them to refine the style. You get to be very selective and specific down to the level of how a particular word is pronounced. No need to be a jerk about it, but you do want to make sure it's right for your book.

SHARE YOUR STORY

My process was absolutely amazing. Critiquing chapter by chapter and getting to hear the story unfold. At one point, I got so excited, I sent my reader a note and ask him to 'hurry up with the next chapter so I could see what was going to happen'. He laughingly reminded me that I was the author. It's just so different to hear it than to read it.

The overall process takes several weeks. It's a lot of work, but a lot of fun. Once everyone's agreed on the final product, much like you did with the paperback and eBook, you'll hit the 'publish' button and you will send it out into the world. In this case, that means to Audible.com and all its related channels.

Unlike the other formats, you do not have any input into the pricing model. It's based on the length of the recording and is controlled by Audible.

As you can tell by my comments along the way, the self publishing route may require a lot of work, but the rewards are pretty amazing. The other thing to note is that, so far, I've mentioned very few costs. Other than the copyright and ISBN, nothing I've done to this point has cost anything but time and effort. When we get into the next few chapters, there will be some opportunities to spend money, but all will be optional.

Meanwhile, as mentioned, for each of the formats, there are multiple companies who can help you to get published. Following is a list of just a few of the links.

https://kdp.amazon.com/self-publishing/signin (E-Book)
https://www.nookpress.com (E-Book)
http://www.smashwords.com/ (E-Book)
https://www.createspace.com/ (Paperback Books)
http://www.lulu.com/ (Paperback and Hardcover Books)
http://www.overdrive.com/#2
http://www1.lightningsource.com/
https://itunesconnect.apple.com
http://www.allromanceebooks.com/
http://www.kobo.com/writinglifehttps://www.acx.com/
http://www.podiobooks.com/ (Podcast-based audiobooks)
http://www.audiobookvoicetalent.com/
http://www.audiofilemagazine.com/gvpages/index.shtml

Chapter 19: Formatting

One of the areas where it may make sense to get outside assistance is formatting. There are two components that require some level of formatting. Those are the Internal Content and the Cover. As with anything, given enough time, patience and the right tools, you can do either of these yourself, but it's at least worth understanding your options.

Internal Content – As discussed in the previous chapter, depending on the publishing service you use, they will provide either templates or guidelines for the formatting of the internal text.

Even with these templates, getting the format just right can take a tremendous amount of time and lots of trial and error. Some of it also comes down to personal preference. I can tell you the basic settings I use, but these are just what I settled on. They are not by any means, a standard.

For my paperbacks, I use line spacing of 1.15 with no space added at the end of a paragraph. I also use size 11 Calibri font. For my Kindles, I use line spacing of 1.00 with no space added at the end of a paragraph and size 10 Arial font. You can tinker with each of these variables to find what is pleasing to your eye.

When I was trying to make these decisions, I polled several published authors I know, and the only consistency was the fact that every one of them had a different combination.

Once these basic settings are determined, then it becomes a game of spacing and indentions to get all the pages to look uniform as a reader thumbs through the book. You do this in two ways.

First, based on what pleases your eye, determine how your chapter breaks will look. What font size will you use for the chapter heading? How far down the page will you place the chapter heading?

Second, by turning on the paragraph tracking mode in the MSWord template and using the markings to make sure that every page is consistent. This can be brutally tedious if you're trying to do the entire book at once.

To my earlier suggestion about writing your book in the template, if you do this, you can also format each chapter as you go. Not only will that save you a ton of time, it will also allow you to see how the book looks as you go. Once again, doing this means that when you type 'the end', the book will be completely formatted and ready for submission.

If the thought of spending hours hitting the tab and enter keys and counting spaces and indentions makes you want to puke, you always have the option to outsource it. On the CreateSpace and Kindle Direct websites, there are 'community' pages. All you have to do is drop a note out there asking for help with formatting and you'll have people respond. You can usually get a book formatted for under $100.

Keep in mind that every time you do a rewrite, you're likely going to have to reformat the book. This could mean multiple fees for the same book.

I've never paid for formatting. Between writing directly into the template and lots of practice, I've managed to get pretty fast with the formatting process. You can too.

Cover – While anyone, with a little effort, can learn to format the internal text, depending on your vision for your book cover, it may take some more specialized skills to get your cover completed.

This is where most people invest some money. Some invest a lot. After all, people really do judge a book by its cover. When you are looking at the cover, there are three areas where you may need some help. They are the Cover Design, Cover Artwork and Cover Formatting.

Cover Design - If you want to give it a shot, you'll need some basic software tools. I managed to create all three of my book cover designs using PowerPoint, but mine were pretty straight forward. Even with that, in all three cases, I either bought stock artwork or I had someone create artwork for me. I'm a writer, not an artist.

The more artistically inclined might be able to use Adobe Photoshop, Adobe Illustrator, Microsoft Paint or GIMP to create the design. It's completely optional.

The basics of Cover Design really boil down to catching a reader's eye and conveying enough about the book to entice them to look further. Some necessities:

- The title and subtitle, if you have one. One pet peeve of mine is people trying to get so cute or artsy that you have to strain to figure out the name of the book. Resist that temptation.
- The name of the author. Don't be afraid to put your name in letters at least equal to the title. After all, there's a better than average chance, a reader will know your name before they know the book's title. Plus, your name is the one constant between all your books.
- A barcode and ISBN number. Usually on the back.
- The title and author's name on the spine of the book.

Beyond those, the possibilities are up to your imagination. Some things to consider.

- A picture of the author. It personalizes the book.
- A bio of the author. This is especially important in nonfiction or if you have a background or expertise that is relevant to the book.
- A synopsis of the book. This is important if your book is being sold in a store where a reader might be browsing.

There are many options when trying to create your design. The most obvious is to use your own imagination to come up with an image, color scheme or graphic. The second option is to find a professional who designs book covers. They are all over the internet or, if you know other authors, get recommendations.

Websites like 99designs, fiverr or mycustombookcover offer a variety of ways to get you connected with multiple designers. If you have ideas, you can share them. If you don't, you can provide them with a book synopsis and let them go to town. Many of these sites have predesigned covers that you can browse through. If you like one, it's usually just a process of changing the text and you're done.

Book cover designs can run the gamut from under a hundred dollars to several hundred dollars. This is a big decision and one where you need to balance cost with professionalism. At the time of my first book, managing cost was high on my list. My expectations of actually selling more than a few copies were low so I didn't want to spend a bunch of money I wasn't going to recoup.

The good news is that I ended up selling far more than I expected. The bad news is that I might have sold even more if I'd spent a little more on the cover design.

A great book cover can be an amazing tool to get people to pick up your book. The story synopsis, reader reviews and possible interactions with you will determine if they actually decide to buy it.

Cover Artwork – I separated the topics of design and artwork simply because, while they might sound like the same thing, they aren't. I created the design for all my book covers and I ultimately did the final formatting for them, but in every case, I either had original artwork created or I bought stock images and manipulated them.

Artwork is exactly what it sounds like. It's the actual image on the cover. Whether it's a hand drawn landscape, a computer graphic of colors and shapes or a photo, there is usually something on the front and back covers that tries to evoke a sense of the book. At the very least, it's there to stir an emotion or catch the eye.

The internet is a great source for images. For all my books, that's where I started. I just searched on google images using the theme of the book. Whether that was gangs, human trafficking or drug abuse, you'd be amazed at the images that you'll find. As your brain registers those images, more ideas will pop.

For two of my books, I took images I found through my web searches and then had them altered to meet my specifications by a professional artist. For my other book, I bought a stock image from

Getty Images and then applied some very basic visual effects to fit the idea in my head.

Just like book cover designers, there are dozens of websites available to get you connected to graphic artists. The internet allows you to find artists from all over the world to bid on your job.

For my first book, *The Victim,* I used a graphic artist in Florida. I sent him a picture from a clothing catalogue, told him I needed it drawn and I gave him a list of details I wanted changed. Add this, delete that, make the background grainy and blue. He was amazing. Literally did it overnight and worked with me for a couple of revisions. I got exactly what I wanted and paid somewhere around $50.

My second book, *Stolen Innocence,* was even easier. I found a photo image that I thought really captured the idea of the book. I paid Getty Images $70 for the use of the photo. I downloaded it from the website, sized it and colored it to match my scheme and then plopped it into the template.

Book number three, *Unseen Carnage,* worked much like the first book. I found a photo that I liked, sent it to a designer in Argentina, told him to hand draw it, taking away a few details and adding a few others. Once again, it was done in days and it cost less than $100.

While I think my current covers are fine, now that I'm a little further down the road, I have considered getting all three redesigned by a professional. I may do that in conjunction with the release of book number four.

Following is a random list of a bunch of cover design and cover art websites that are out there. I'm not recommending or endorsing any of them. It's just a starting point.

      http://bookcovers.creativindie.com/
      http://booksat.scarlettrugers.com/
      http://www.candescentpress.com
      http://coverart.joleenenaylor.com/
      http://digitaldonna.com/
      http://flipcitybooks.com/

SHARE YOUR STORY

Formatting – The final step in the cover process is the formatting. With each type of format, paperback, eBook or audio, the company you're using for printing and distribution will have its own standards and specifications for the cover.

In most cases, they will provide you with a template to use to make sure that the cover will fit the book. Beyond that, the two other fairly consistent requirements were that you provide the final artwork in pdf format and that any images be at least 300 dpi. That's a requirement that you can provide to your designer or graphic artist and they will provide the master files to meet that specification.

Formatting itself is pretty straight forward. I did all of mine in PowerPoint. If you don't have the tools or don't know how to use them, you can find someone who does either through your local writer's group or a basic google search.

Chapter 20:
Sales and Marketing

Do you feel your skin starting to crawl yet? Usually just mentioning the word Sales to a writer makes them shudder. After all, you signed up to write the next great American novel, you didn't sign up to 'sell' books.

I know. I've been involved in the sales process in the consulting world for most of my career and I still insist that I'm not a 'sales guy'. If it makes you feel any better, don't think of it as sales, think of it as providing someone with the opportunity to have their life changed by your book.

Even if your book is the fluffiest fiction on the planet, if it's good and it's entertaining, then you've brought some level of joy into the readers' world. Why would you ever want to avoid bringing a little joy into someone's life?

While in most cases, people associate Marketing with the advertisement of a product and Sales with the specific act of taking an order. In the book word, the lines are more blurred. Other than the times you do a direct book signing event or unless you own a book store, it will be rare when you will directly sell your book to someone.

In the world of books, all the Marketing and Sales efforts are really designed to get you, your story and your book in front of the right people at the right time. Keep in mind, there are literally billions of people on earth who read. If a book sells a few hundred thousand copies, it's considered an enormous hit. In fact, most books, regardless of publishing route or channel, are considered successful if they merely sell in the thousands.

My point is that all you need to do to be successful is to reach a tiny fraction of the overall market. To do this, it's all about visibility. In fact, one book I'd recommend is called Let's Get Visible by David Gaughran. It's focused specifically on eBooks and Amazon and it goes deep in the weeds about how to position your book using key words and categories and how to play the algorithms.

But there's more to marketing than Search Engine Optimization and my objective in this chapter is to expose you to several different tools, options and avenues you can pursue. You can choose to do none of them or all of them. Whichever path or paths you go down, you will be able to find much more detail on each individual route just by searching.

Before we jump into the various paths, it's worth taking a moment to think about your objective. Are you writing for fun? Are you writing to stir action? Are you writing to make a living?

The answers to these questions will directly impact the level of effort you put into your marketing strategy as well as the types of marketing tools you use. I'm going to try to sequence the following few pages to scale from the very basics to the hard core. In other words, even if you are writing just for the fun of it and so that your grandkids can have something to remember you by, there are a few steps you'll want to take that will at least get the book out there so that there is a chance someone might buy it.

On Line Retailer – Whether it's Amazon, Barnes and Noble or other on line outlets, there are a few components that are required. The level of attention you pay to these components will directly impact the number of readers you attract and the number of books you sell.

The very first component is your book title. While this is important in fiction, it's absolutely critical in nonfiction. In fiction, it needs to be catchy and appealing to that genre's readers. It should have some connection with the story and at least hint at the topic. In nonfiction, the title and subtitle may be the most important component because they lay out the subject matter of the book. If you read the title and subtitle of this book, it's clear that it's a book about 'how to write and publish a book'. If you as a reader, aren't interested in writing a book, the chances of you going any further in your investigation of this book are almost zero.

For nonfiction, while you want to be catchy, don't outthink yourself to the point of confusing people about the content of the book. I'm a big fan of the author / entrepreneur Tim Ferriss. He has a series of books that are focused on self-improvement. Each title starts with 'The Four Hour...'. The Four Hour Workweek was first. The second was the Four Hour Body. The third was the Four Hour Chef. From those titles, the topics seem obvious. The first book is about productivity, the second book is about working out and the third book is a cookbook, right? Well, you'd be right for the first two. The third one, while it is structured around learning to cook, it's really about the process of learning. Based on numerous comments he's made on his podcast, I sense he regrets the title decision for book number three. The market for cookbooks is very different than the market for learning analysis.

There may be very scientific ways of choosing a title, but I'd suggest the old fashioned way. Get input from friends, family and colleagues. Come up with alternatives and just ask people what they think. Never forget, though, this is your book and you have to be happy with the title and it has to be a title you can live with forever.

We've talked already at some length about the second component. The cover is critical for catching people's attention and conveying a sense of the book. Same as with the title, get several opinions, but remember it's your book.

The third component is the synopsis. This is critical. When you are shopping for books on line or in the book store, what is the one thing you always do? You read the synopsis. If that isn't interesting, you won't buy the book. Do not underestimate the synopsis. Spend the appropriate amount of time on it. Get others to read it. Treat it the same way you treat the book content. Once someone has decided to pick up the book (i.e. they liked the cover and the title), what they read in the synopsis will determine if they move forward.

Give enough of the story so they can get a sense of where it's going, but also include some of the conflict, the issues and the theme. If there is a message, at least hint at it enough to get people curious. Don't try to give it all away. This may be a synopsis, but it's also a tease. Think of it as being a movie trailer.

The fourth component is something you've already done, but now you need to look at it in a new light. Chapter One seals the deal. Most online retailers allow the shopper to read all or part of Chapter One. If you spend all of Chapter One talking about the pretty mountains or the beautiful streams and you never get around to telling the reader what the book is about, no one will buy the book. This is where the chapter ending is so important. If the reader isn't asking, 'what happens next' when that chapter ends, they won't buy the book.

Those four components – Title, Cover, Synopsis, Chapter One – are really the basic table stakes. Take the time to make sure you've done everything you can to make them as interesting and appealing as possible. All the online marketing and social media in the world won't sell books if those four components aren't solid.

There is one other component that is important, but I separate it out because you have very little control over it. That component is reader reviews. Sure, you can have your mom, sister and best friend all go write five star reviews. You can even be sleazy and pay people to write five star reviews. But in the end, those reviews are going to be unveiled as fraudulent if, when real readers post, they give you one star reviews.

The thrill of getting a five star review from a complete stranger is something I hope each of you gets to experience at least once. It's a high that few other experiences can touch. Of course, getting a bad review, or even just fearing a bad review, can be soul crushing. To be an author, you need thick skin. No matter how good you write, there's going to be someone who will say disparaging things about it.

My advice is simply to believe in your product and let the chips fall where they may. I ask every reader to post a review. Very few actually do. I've been fortunate so far that the readers who have taken the time to post, have been very complimentary.

The importance of the review is twofold. The sheer number of reviews is a clear indication of how many people have read the book. If I see several hundred reviews, I instinctively know that several thousand people have read the book. If I only see five reviews, my mind assumes they've sold very few books. As a reader, subconsciously, I'm going to be drawn to the book that has sold more copies.

The actual rating (i.e. 4.8 out of 5.0 stars) is clearly important, but also loses a certain amount of value if you don't have enough reviews. The cynic in all of us will tend to think that if you only have five reviews, that most of them are from friends and family. After all, if you can't get at least five buddies to write reviews, you probably need to reevaluate your circle of friends.

Like most readers, I'll mentally rank a book with an average of 4.0 stars but with five hundred reviews, higher than a book with an average of 4.5 stars but only five reviews. The assumption is that the five hundred reviewers cover a much larger sample of society and are less likely to have a personal connection to the author.

Bottom line is to get as many reviews as you possibly can even if that means the average rating might be slightly lower.

Website / Profile Pages – Although not required by any means, the next lowest hanging fruit is creating a website or at the very least creating profile pages.

Websites used to be very complicated and extremely expensive. They are neither nowadays. You can get your own domain for a few dollars a month and most hosting services provide basic templates for you to build out your content.

In its simplest form, all you're trying to do with a website is to give readers a place to go where they can learn more about you and about your books. If you can provide information about upcoming events, a link for them to click on to buy your books and a way for them to leave their email address and comments, all the better.

You can get all kinds of crazy with a website as far as design goes. The sky's the limit on how much time, effort and money you can spend. Before you drop several thousand dollars though, ask yourself how often you've visited the website of your favorite author. Once? Did the graphics really make you want to buy their book? I didn't think so.

SHARE YOUR STORY

Two of the big players in the website game are godaddy and wix. Both provide templates and tools that allow you to literally go from zero to functioning website in a few hours. The technology is simple and easy to use and if you keep it basic, it's cheap.

As an alternative or supplement to a website, you can also create profile pages on multiple sites. The two biggest are Amazon and Goodreads. Creating an author page and profile on either site can be done in less than an hour.

The benefit of those site profiles is that they are resident on the platforms where the readers spend their time. If I'm on Amazon or Goodreads already, clicking on a link to see an Authors' profile is quick and easy and I don't have to leave the site. Actually going to an Authors' website means leaving the site and venturing into the unknown.

Depending on your desire for exposure, my recommendation is to do both. Create a simple website of your own and make sure that you have a profile on as many reader sites as possible.

Everything I've touched on so far is really the basics for anyone who wants to sell books beyond their family and friends. The effort and costs involved to this point have been minimal.

Let's take the next step.

Social Media – Since the world of Social Media changes every day and some new app is the latest craze every month, I'm not going to try to be exhaustive with which forms of Social Media to use. I'm going to stick with the household names and just assume that you can expand this conversation to include the latest and greatest app.

The two big dogs of Social Media are FaceBook and Twitter. You should plan to be on both. On either, you can choose to have both personal pages as well as author pages.

Neither platform charges money, but both can be a terrible time suck if you're not careful. They also both have the potential to do as much damage as good. In this day and age of vitriolic politics, race and religion, you should assume that anything you post that is the least bit controversial is going to piss off half your potential readers.

As we all advise our teenagers, don't post anything that you wouldn't want your parents to read. Furthermore, don't post anything that's going to chase potential readers away.

The best use of both FaceBook and Twitter is simply as a means to let people know you exist, to let them know that you write and to entice them to look at your books. It's great for letting people know about upcoming events or about the pending release of your next book. I've seen people use FaceBook to drum up interest in the 'cover reveal' for a new book.

The best advice is to post regularly. If you don't have anything to post about your books, post book recommendations. If you don't have any upcoming events, post on behalf of authors you know. The real point is to stay on your reader's radar while you work on your next book.

If you are a nonfiction writer and you want to get people talking about your book's topic, both platforms allow you that opportunity. Be warned that almost any topic these days can be politicized and once that genie is out of the bottle, putting it back in is essentially impossible. Posts on Social Media last longer than dinosaur bones.

Finally, although I personally find this a bit annoying, the publishing and advertising worlds do pay attention to the number of followers and friends you have. If you are trying to get a traditional publishing deal and you have one hundred followers, good luck. If you have a million, grab you pen.

Personal Appearances – Now comes the fun stuff. Getting to interact directly with readers who are buying your book or who have already read your book is about the coolest experience on the planet. I've found very few authors who don't love to talk to readers. After all, humans of all kinds crave validation, and authors aren't any different.

Hearing someone tell you they loved your book is pretty cool. Getting into a real discussion about the topics in the book, how the characters developed and where you came up with your ideas is even better.

There are really three forums for reader interaction – Book Signings, Book Club Discussions and Speaking Engagements. All of those overlap to a certain extent, but they can be independent of each other.

Book signings usually occur at a book store or some other type of organization that is willing to host you and allow you to set up a table where you can sell and sign your books. Often, they will schedule it so that you can speak to the audience for a few minutes and then sit at a table, sign books and take pictures. It's an amazing ego pump. It's also a terrific way to meet your readers and get their direct feedback. The one thing I've learned is that readers aren't shy about expressing their opinions.

Book clubs work in a similar fashion, they are just a little more exclusive and you'll have a more captive audience. The nice thing about book clubs is that they are usually very avid readers and want to really talk about the story, characters, plots and themes. You'll need to be on the ball when talking with them. There's a good chance they will know your books better than you do.

Speaking engagements are the more formal version of the book club and book signing. Nonfiction books lend themselves to speaking engagements a little more than fiction simply because nonfiction books address topics about which people want to get educated. Unless your fictional book dives deep into a theme or topic to which you can speak intelligently, it may be hard to book true speaking engagements.

All three have a couple of things in common. First, you need to be comfortable in front of a crowd. That can be difficult even for someone with an outgoing personality. Talking to groups can be intimidating and if you are brought in for a formal speaking engagement, you'll need to have a rehearsed speech ready.

Second, they will require a little hustle and self-promotion in order to get them booked. It's a bit like the chicken and the egg. If you haven't sold any books, it's hard to get personal appearances booked. If you can't get personal appearances booked, it's hard to sell books.

Local book stores, if you can find one, are great for book signings. You can negotiate with them on what percentage they will get off the sale of each book. It's usually anywhere from 25% to 40%. My objective with personal appearances is to get new readers. If I make money, that's a bonus. I've done book signings at book stores, grocery stores, restaurants and even a brewery. As long as people show up, they are a blast.

JOE B. PARR

Marketing Material – If you are going to do any kind of personal appearances, you will need the basic items associated with setting up a booth or table. This usually includes some level of banners, posters, flyers, bookmarks, business cards and possibly some form of giveaway items. You'll likely also need a table, table cloth, chair and basic office supplies.

My first suggestion before you buy anything, is to go to several book signings and just scope out what others are doing. You'll find that it runs the gamut from a bare table with books sitting on it, to multiple banners and flashing lights. You'll also find that each individual item can be professionally designed with amazing logos and graphics to homemade posters and signs.

Once again, basic software tools like PowerPoint and Adobe Photoshop can be used to accomplish almost anything you want to produce. Your individual artistic design skills will probably be the limiting factor. As with the cover design and artwork, you can hire someone to develop the design. In fact, quite often, the same artist that designed you cover can design your banners, posters and bookmarks. After all, you'll likely want them to have the same look and feel.

Once you have a design, getting them produced is straight forward. Online printers such as Vistaprint and Printrunner do very good work and deliver within days. If you need something done in hours instead of days, Fedex Office can accommodate, but is usually more expensive. There are also any number of local printshops.

The table, chair, bookstands and office supplies can be bought at any office supply store like OfficeMax, WalMart or Costco.

As with everything we've talked about, you have two tradeoffs – Cost versus Time. How much can you do yourself and want to do yourself to save money versus how fast and fancy do you want it to be?

As for marketing giveaways, you can have your logo, image or book title printed on just about anything from coffee mugs to ink pens. Some of the companies I've already mentioned have those capabilities, but there are others that focus specifically on imprinting. On line companies like 4imprint, leaderpromos and qualitylogoproducts are just a few of the options.

SHARE YOUR STORY

Other than bookmarks, I've never done any marketing giveaways, but I know authors who do it regularly. It's all about building a connection with your readers. If having an ink pen with your name on it helps that process, then go for it.

For those that want to take your book sales beyond the people with whom you can personally connect level, there are several avenues you can take. Let's explore those.

Local Press – Another option for visibility that takes a little hustle and self-promotion is the local press. These days, almost every city has some sort of local magazine, either online or in print. They are always looking for local citizens that are doing something interesting and most people consider publishing a book to be interesting.

It usually takes finding a copy of the publication and reading it to find the publisher or editor. Most of the time their contact information will be provided. You can reach out to them either by phone or email. My one piece of advice is to have your story down. They get hit up twenty times a day by people wanting to have an article written about the son, daughter or pet.

Be ready to tell them about your book, your background and why their readers should be interested. You should also be ready to write most, if not all the article that will get published. You'll need to get past any issues you may have with tooting your own horn.

Advertising – While taking out traditional ads in newspapers or magazines is an option that may make sense for the traditionally published author, I've never seen self published authors go that route. The option is there.

A more viable advertising route may be online advertising. FaceBook, Twitter, Goodreads and many other Social Media platforms offer ad space in the form of side, top or bottom banners. The ads are not overly expensive. You can run ads for as little as $50. My experience with them is that they also aren't overly effective.

While it's not exactly advertisement, you can leverage some of the marketing capabilities with Amazon with various price promotions. One specific program is the Kindle Countdown. This is where you can establish a promotional price for a block of time and Kindle Direct will list your book on the Kindle Countdown site. You can do some targeted advertisement through websites like The Fussy Librarian. For a small fee, if your book meets some basic qualifications, you can have your book listed on their daily or weekly email blasts that go out to their email list. That has the potential to reach more than ten thousand readers at one point. Combining an email blast like that with a Kindle Countdown promotion can be impactful and very cost conscious.

There's a level of marketing that is very focused on direct outreach to your reader community and providing them with multiple ways to interact with you. Let's talk about some of those options.

Blog – A very natural extension of your writing is to create and write a daily, weekly or monthly blog. Essentially, this is just a short written post on a blogsite or your website.

You have complete freedom to write about any topic that comes to mind. Typically, authors will write about something that is relevant to their books. Because of that, this is a tool that is more often used by nonfiction writers than novelists.

The entries don't have to be long or overly profound. Readers just like to hear from authors if they are interested in the topic or if they enjoy reading the author's books.

Setting up a blog will cost a few dollars a month and can be done through your website hosting company. There are also companies that specialize in hosting blogs such as wordpress.

Not only is this a great way to stay in front of your readers and to interact with your readers, it's also a great way to collect email addresses. More on that in a moment.

Podcast – If you have speaking skills that lend themselves to being recorded, another option is publishing a podcast. Again, because it requires publishing on a weekly or monthly basis and by definition, requires new content for each podcast, it's often more applicable to nonfiction writers than to novelists.

Very similar to a blog, a podcast needs to be hosted. This can be in conjunction with your website or through a number of podcast hosting organizations. Sites like pantheon, buzzsprout and podbean are just a few options.

SHARE YOUR STORY

Beyond having a place to host the podcast, you will also need a way to distribute the podcast. In most cases, you will have multiple distributors. The biggest name is iTunes but there are dozens of podcast apps that can be downloaded.

In addition to hosting and distribution of the final, produced podcast, you will also need to have the tools and capability to record each session. This will require both hardware and software that is specifically designed for podcasts. These aren't terribly expensive, but if you've never dealt with audio recording programs and software, you will likely need to take some time to get educated.

Recording audio files, transforming them and uploading will take patience and time. If you need to have guests who will be interviewed via phone, that requires additional equipment and software. The good news is that there are numerous resources, articles and books on the topic. If you're interested, do your research. Much like everything else I've covered, there's a balance between how much effort you expend and how much money you spend.

YouTubing – Going the next step... Instead of just audio, you can add video and publish it via YouTube. Much like podcasting, if you plan to post videos on a regular basis, you'll need to have topics and / or guests. You'll also need to have digital video recording equipment and a good enough internet connection to upload large video files.

The fun side of either podcasting or youtubing is that your readers get an opportunity to see a different side of you than they might get through reading your books or your blog. I know I always enjoy seeing the personality of my favorite authors. It's often very different than you expected.

BookTubing – There is a whole community centered around YouTube where avid book readers have their own YouTube channels where they discuss books. It can range from general discussions to book reviews to paid book advertisements.

Much like the various book review websites, it centers around how many subscribers they have for their YouTube channel. I've never attempted to get my books reviewed by a BookTuber, so I don't know exactly how that process works. My assumption is that you could contact the BookTuber through their YouTube page and ask them how it works.

All of these options are different ways to stay in front of your readers and they all give you various reasons for connecting with your readers.

Email Lists – The final piece to the puzzle may be the holy grail of all the options. Any time you interact with a reader, whether it's getting them to visit your website, meeting them at a book signing, book club or speaking engagement or having them read your blog, listen to your podcast or watch your YouTube video, one of your primary goals should be to get their email address to add to your list.

Having the ability to reach out to hundreds or thousands of readers with a single push of a button is invaluable. When you are having an event, or releasing a new book, there's no better tool than a direct email to the reader.

There are several tools you can use. One of the easiest is MailChimp. It allows you up to two thousand email addresses for free and provides you with the ability to create content using predefined templates, to include pictures as well as text and to send test emails before you send the blast to the whole list. It's incredibly easy to use.

The value of an email list cannot be understated. As you grow and move from author to blogger to podcaster to online entrepreneur, you have a built in audience that you can access directly. Kevin Kelly of Wired magazine wrote a great article about how you can build a business based on just one thousand loyal subscribers. While it may not be specifically applicable to authors, it's well worth a read.

I hope I've convinced you that Sales and Marketing are not dirty words and I hope I've shown you that it's really up to you regarding how much time, effort and money you spend. My suggestion is to try a few different approaches and find the ones with which you are comfortable.

They can all be a level of work, but they can also all be a lot of fun. Speaking to a group of avid readers is a blast. Getting to sign autographs will blow your mind. Even just seeing your name or the title of your book on a bookmark, poster, banner or coffee mug will most likely make you smile.

SHARE YOUR STORY

Just remember, if you're true underlying objective is to connect with readers and to bring them information, entertainment or joy, then just hop on and go for the ride. The wind blowing through your hair will be refreshing.

Go Tell Your Story:

One question I asked my authors was, when did they first 'realize' they had earned the title of author?

"When I held the galley copy of Phoenix in my hands. When I flipped it open and saw my words on the paper. I cried in the CVS parking lot." – Kimberly Packard

"Seeing it live on Amazon and B&N. With my name, by Susan Sheehey next to it. That was the moment." – Susan Sheehey

"I believe anyone who writes is an author. They created something. 'Author' doesn't mean 'published', it means 'created'. Although, signing that first paperback was pretty awesome." – C.A. Szarek

My Great Grandmother lived to be almost 102 years old. Antonia Parr came to America from Germany in the late 1880's. She actually came over once, landed in Baltimore, got homesick and returned to Germany. Then came back a year later, landed in New York and traveled to Kansas to meet up with her father. Both trips were by ship. She was seventeen at the time.

She went on to experience an amazing life that included living in Kansas, North Dakota, Idaho, Utah and finally Texas. All this bouncing around was done while raising a large family and traveling by covered wagon and train. She was a true pioneer woman who ate prairie dog soup with the Sioux Indians and at different times, owned and ran a saloon, a hotel, a butcher shop and multiple farms.

Through it all, if you'd have asked her, she'd have told you she was just an ordinary person doing what she needed to do to survive and raise a family in a harsh new land. She never viewed her life as anything

SHARE YOUR STORY

exotic or exciting or special.

Why am I sharing this? For two reasons. First, I only know all of this because my great grandmother took the time, while she was bored in the old folk's home, to write a series of letters to my father's cousin (a nun in a convent). This series of letters was essentially her life's story. I've read these letters multiple times with the awe and interest of reading a best-selling thriller. Second, it's a great illustration of someone who had no idea that her story would be so incredibly fascinating. Yet, when told decades later, it sounds like a movie script.

Everybody has a story. You may not have crossed the American Wilderness in a covered wagon with six kids in the back, but you've done something, achieved something, experienced something or survived something that someone, somewhere will find interesting.

So, how do you figure out what story to tell? What is YOUR story? The truth is, you probably have multiple stories that, when combined, make up your universe. Sometimes those stories are about you personally. Other times, those stories are about the people around you who shaped and influenced you. My great grandmother's story is very much a part of my story. We're connected by heritage, but more importantly, her decisions and experiences shaped the lives of my grandfather and my father and ultimately were the reason I was born and raised in Fort Worth, TX.

Don't discount your story. It may be funny, or inspirational, or simply tragic. But if you can extract the nuances, the underlying themes and convey the emotional impact of what happened, your story will resonate with readers.

At the end of the day, the reader wants to go on a journey. They want to feel the highs and lows. They want to be surprised and captivated. They want to wonder how it's going to end. And they want to nod knowingly when it's done.

You can take them on that journey with your story.

Go Share Your Story.

Acknowledgements

Unlike most books that start as original little story seeds in the back of your mind and are slowly watered and cultivated over time to blossom into a novel, this book was the result of taking a personal journey and discovering a passion.

Just like any journey, none of these words would have stumbled onto the pages without the help, guidance and direction from a number of fellow authors, friends and family.

The first person who needs to be acknowledged is Clover Autrey. My initial glimpse into the world of self publishing was provided when she presented at a meeting of the Greater Fort Worth Writers group. She provided an outline of notes, suggestions and hints about the process which I leveraged liberally during the writing of this book. Clover is a Fort Worth based Romance Novelists with at least twelve titles in print.

My eloquent panel of authors who not only willingly provided answers to my questions and quotes for this book, they were also the team that provided direction, help and encouragement to me throughout the process of writing and publishing my first three novels.

Following are their profiles. Check out their books. They're great.

C.A. Szarek is a USA Today Bestselling, award winning author of romantic suspense, epic and historical fantasy romance, C.A. loves to dabble in different genres. If it's a good story, she'll write it, no matter where it seems to fit!

She's a hopeless romantic and always will be. Risking it all for Happily Ever After is what she lives by!

SHARE YOUR STORY

C.A. is originally from Ohio, but got to Texas as soon as she could. She's happily married and has a bachelor's degree in Criminal Justice.

She works with kids when she's not writing.

You can find her through the following links:

www.caszarek.com

Facebook: http://www.facebook.com/caszarek

Blog: http://www.caszarekwriter.blogspot.com

Twitter & Instagram: @caszarek

Kimberly Packard is an award-winning author of women's fiction. She began visiting her spot on the shelves at libraries and bookstores at a young age, gazing between the Os and the Qs. Kimberly received a degree in journalism from the University of North Texas, and has worked in public relations and communications for nearly 20 years.

When she isn't writing, she can be found running, doing a poor imitation of yoga or curled up with a book. She resides in North Texas with her husband Colby, a clever cat named Oliver and a yellow lab named Charlie.

Her debut novel, Phoenix, was awarded as Best General Fiction of 2013 by the Texas Association of Authors. Other published works by Kimberly include a Christmas novella, The Crazy Yates. The sequel to Phoenix, Pardon Falls, is due for release in January 2018 and the final book in the trilogy, Prospera Pass, in late 2018.

You can find her through the following links:

www.kimberlypackard.com

Facebook: http:// www.facebook.com/kimberlypackardauthor

Twitter & Instagram: @kimberlypackard

Susan Sheehey writes contemporary romance, romantic suspense and women's fiction. Water plays a crucial element in all of her novels, and she's a strong advocate for Autism Awareness. Forced to give up Diet Coke, she now functions on heavy amounts of French Vanilla coffee. Susan lives and laughs in Texas with her husband and two sons. Escape in romance and suspense!

You can find her at through the following links:
www.SusanSheehey.com
Facebook – https://www.facebook.com/susansheehey
Twitter and Instagram: @susieqwriter
Bookbub: https://www.bookbub.com/authors/susan-sheehey

Jeffrey Thomas Bacot resides in Fort Worth, Texas and has spent the majority of his life in the Metroplex area. He graduated from Southern Methodist University in 1985 with a BA in Political Science and a BBA in Business Finance and received and graduate degree in banking in 1997. Jeff spent 25 years in banking as SVP of commercial lending for 4 banks. He has been a full time writer since 2010. He has written two published books ("On the Hole" and a non-fiction on banking) as well as two unpublished books, twelve short stories and a monthly blog- *Wrongs To Write: Defying Fiction Conviction*. His primary genre is literary fiction, but he has also written sports stories, business stories and general fiction.

Jeff is an avid sportsman and plays golf regularly. He writes the majority of his work from his loft in downtown Fort Worth. He speaks French fluently and travels to France annually for research, writing and pleasure.

He can be contacted at www.jeffbacot.com.

Ken Ingle quit the professional world in June 1996, after having owned a company, served as Executive VP, and as President of another, in order to write. The former Navy man, father of three, grandfather of six, and two great-grandsons, has published ten novels, seven science fiction, and three mysteries.

Ken qualified as member of the Sixth Naval District Pistol Team and toured extensively. He is a licensed pilot. The city streets were well known to him. All of these have been a great help in developing ideas for his novels.

According to Ken: "I've experienced love, hate, violence, peace, failure, and success giving me a wealth of experience from which to draw and develop ideas and plots." He now lives in Arlington, TX.

SHARE YOUR STORY

Chris Crawford is a writer of speculative fiction and the former president of Greater Forth Worth Writers. His first novel, THE TUNING STATION, was released in 2015. ACROSS HEAVEN AND HELL, the first book of the Ro and Jules series, will be released in 2018. For his day job he's a software engineer. He currently lives in Texas with his wife Jennifer, three sons and two cats.

You can find Chris at:

URL: https://www.chrisacrawford.com
Twitter: @crawwriter
Facebook: https://www.facebook.com/ChrisACrawfordAuthor/

In addition to these fantastic authors, the love and support of my wife Greta and my daughters Caitlin and Aubrey were invaluable throughout the process of researching and writing this book. I am, as always, forever grateful.

Thanks to all.

www.ingramcontent.com/pod-product-compliance
Lightning Source LLC
Chambersburg PA
CBHW031451040426
42444CB00007B/1061